Open Client/Server Computing and Middleware

Open Client/Server Computing and Middleware

Alan R. Simon
Tom Wheeler

AP PROFESSIONAL

Boston San Diego New York
London Sydney Tokyo Toronto

Copyright © 1995 by Academic Press, Inc.

AP PROFESSIONAL
1300 Boylston St., Chestnut Hill, MA 02167

An Imprint of ACADEMIC PRESS, INC.
A Division of HARCOURT BRACE & COMPANY

United Kingdom Edition published by
ACADEMIC PRESS LIMITED
24–28 Oval Road, London NW1 7DX

Simon, Alan R.
  Open client / server computing and middleware / Alan R. Simon, Tom
  Wheeler.
        p.   cm.
    Includes index.
    ISBN 0-12-643860-9
    Client /server computing. 2. middleware. I. Wheeler, Thomas
  F. II. Title.
  QA76.76.M54S55 1995
  004'.36--dc20   95-9514
                                                    CIP

Printed in the United States of America
  95 96 97 98   ML   9 8 7 6 5 4 3 2 1

Contents

PART II CASE STUDY 1 55

APPENDICES 221

Preface

In 1992, I began the process of updating the late Tom Wheeler's *Open Systems Handbook* to a second edition, now published by AP Professional (1994). At the same time, I undertook to complete his second work, now titled *Open Client/Server Computing and Middleware.* Those two books, along with my own *Network Re-Engineering: Foundations of Enterprise Computing* (1994) form a three-volume set, which will provide a solid foundation in the world of open, scalable, client/server computing environments.

About the contents of this book . . . When I originally agreed to complete Tom's manuscript, it was apparent how much had changed in the client/server world even in the past few years. The euphoria of the late 1980s and early 1990s ("The PC will replace the mainframe! All computing applications and systems will be developed effortlessly, cheaply, and be easy to maintain using client/server technology!") had given way to a hard, realistic look at the deficiencies and shortcomings of client/server technology and architectures. In 1993, we saw the growth of the "middleware movement" and what has become known as "second-generation client/server architectures."

In short, I faced a bit of a puzzle regarding how to proceed with this book. My first cut was a survey of a variety of different visual development environments and middleware technologies and products, but what became evident was that the landscape was moving much too quickly to get a snapshot that was both broad enough and deep enough to be a definitive "encyclopedia" of middleware technology and next-generation open client/server computing. Many of the technologies and products I had originally planned to include had fallen out of favor or, in some cases, faded away altogether.

What emerged, then, was the book in its present form. The first part deals with the historic roots of client/server computing, providing a foundation for both the architectural discussions in that section and the case studies in the following chapters of the book. Instead of, for example, discussing the Distributed Computing Environment (DCE) in an in-depth manner (this can be found in many other excellent DCE books) or debating the merits of the various object management models (COM, SOM), it was decided that it would be much more valuable for the reader if we presented an in-depth set of case studies about two different open client/server development environments—one on Microsoft Windows, the other about UNIX—and discuss the architectures, various product components and how they interrelate, and present case study examples of *how these things really work.*

One of the things that I have had to keep in mind with respect to much of my writing and particularly for this book is that it's easy, being a writer and consultant focusing on emerging technologies, to assume that "sure, everyone knows about visual development, database stored procedures, multitiered client/server architectures. . . ." In reality, many computing professionals, including a large portion of the readers of this book, are still primarily involved in mainframe, 3GL (e.g., COBOL) application development and have not had exposure to visual development, client/server architectures and the other topics covered in the case studies in this book. What I've tried to do is give a tutorial-oriented overview of two different environments and present the computer professional—*any* computer professional—with a concise snapshot of how client/server computing is being done today and will be done for the next few years.

Alan Simon
February 1995

Acknowledgments

I am grateful to the staff at both Bluestone (Mt. Laurel, NJ) and ProtoView Development Corporation (Dayton, NJ) for their assistance with this book. They were kind enough to spend a great deal of time with me, demonstrating their products and providing the support needed to make this book a reality.

PART I

Overview

1

Open Systems and Client/Server Computing: An Overview

INTRODUCTION

In this chapter, we'll take a brief look at the concepts of open systems and client/server computing, focusing on the roots of these two related trends in the quest for cost-effective, flexible information technology solutions. This chapter is adapted from a companion volume to this book, *Network Re-Engineering: Foundations of Enterprise Computing.*[1] For additional detailed information about open systems technology, the reader is directed to another companion volume, *Open Systems Handbook*, 2d edition.[2]

WHAT ARE OPEN SYSTEMS?

Many information systems (IS) professionals understandably confuse the concepts and implementations of open systems, enterprise computing, and client/server computing with one another. All areas are relatively new in name (i.e., all were born in the mid-1980s and have matured more or less in lockstep with one another), although their respective concepts have been goals of computing environments for many years.

Additionally, within the realm of open systems, there is even more confusion. Many computer professionals—particularly those with batch mainframe backgrounds who are looking at broadening their skills

3

base—are surprised to learn that there are multiple variants of the UNIX operating system and that the POSIX they may have read about is not the same as UNIX per se, but, in fact, transcends basic operating systems functionality. They may also be surprised to learn that there is not one "open systems" movement and related consortia, but several competing ones. Also, there is a great deal of disharmony in the open systems consortium and vendor world. Further, the various consortia have undergone mergers and consolidations in recent years, adding to the confusion.

Part of the problem begins with the precise definition—or lack thereof—of open systems. One consulting manager was quoted in the early 1990s in a trade periodical as saying, "I define open systems the way some people define obscenity: I can't define it, but I know it when I see it."[3] Tongue-in-cheek definitions aside, there are multiple ways to define open systems.

Open systems arguably had its beginning in the late 1970s with the Open Systems Interconnect (OSI) network protocols standards effort, which arose in competition to IBM's dominance with its Systems Network Architecture (SNA).[4]

The open systems movement got a boost from the rising popularity of the UNIX operating system. Despite the variants of UNIX (initially System V and Berkeley, and later OSF and others), it was still easier to port software between and interconnect UNIX systems than, say, IBM VM and Honeywell GCOS mainframes.

A further definition of open systems, in the context of OSI, UNIX, and other efforts, is echoed as "interfaces [that] are open in the sense that they are readily available to anyone in the industry who would choose to implement them."[5]

Others believe that "open systems" has grown to be nothing more than a "politically correct" term with little or no substance, evolving from an "honorable and sincere attempt to define common standards where they made sense" into "another item of marketing baggage."[6]

Regardless of what definition (or lack thereof) one chooses to use with respect to open systems, the fact remains that open systems are very important in the context of enterprise computing. It stands to reason that the more "open" the required base technology components of information systems architectures are, the easier it is to connect vast amounts of computing resources to create an enterprise environment. Every base technology area that is now crucial to complex information processing architectures—databases, user interfaces, interoperability services, networking and communications services, and so on—has an "open" flavor to it that either complements or supersedes its proprietary history. Electronic mail and directory services have X.400 and X.500; networks have the OSI reference model; databases and repositories have the SQL and IRDS standards, as well as open interoperability mechanisms; and so on. Modern applications all have an open flavor to them through the use of APIs, common services, user interfaces, and so forth. Each of the vendor or consortium enterprise architectures is oriented around open, public interface and application mechanisms.

ENTERPRISE COMPUTING AND OPEN SYSTEMS

Continuing with the last thought—enterprise computing and open systems—what are the distinctions between the two?

Open systems are oriented towards an environment where most or all of the computing technology that comprises that environment is based upon standards, regardless of the scope of the environment: departmental or organization-wide. Enterprise computing, by contrast, encompasses not only open systems concepts but, by virtue of existing environments that must be incorporated as well, a great deal of proprietary interfaces and interoperability mechanisms (see Figure 1.1).

In the early 1990s, as both movements were beginning to gain momentum, there was some degree of overlap between open systems and enterprise computing, the amount of which was hindered somewhat by the stage at which enterprise architectures and standards were. It was anticipated that over time, as the enterprise architectures, open standards, and products built on one or both evolved and matured, the gap between the two would narrow and a greater degree of overlap would occur (Figure 1.2).[7] As it turns out, the two movements have converged on one another somewhat faster than had been envisioned only a few years ago (see Figure 1.3). Part of the reason is that the linchpin of enterprise computing, the vendor-driven architectures such as IBM's SAA, didn't take hold to the degree that the vendors would have liked. At the same time, the "weak link" of the open systems world—overly ambitious, horrendously complex standards—caused open systems practitioners to look for alternatives to the "wonderful world of standards," and those alternatives were often found in enterprise-oriented solutions, such as software bridges and gateways.

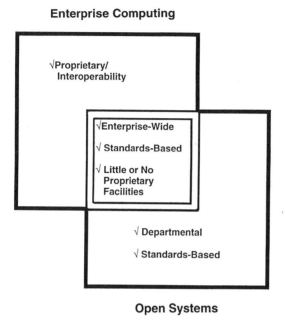

Figure 1.1 Respective characteristics of open systems and enterprise computing

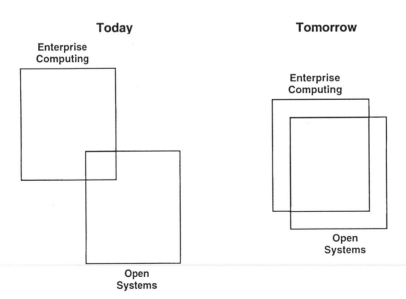

Figure 1.2 Present and future relationship between open systems and enterprise computing

Open Systems Standards	Enterprise Architectures
• Multiple Standards Efforts	• Committee–Developed to Satisfy Multiple Groups within a Vendor
• Committee–Developed to Satisfy Multiple Vendors	
• Politically Influenced	• Politically Influenced
• Not All-Encompassing	• Not All-Encompassing
• Products Slow to Appear	• Products Slow to Appear
• Heterogeneous Interoperability Products Still Required	• Heterogeneous Interoperability Products Still Required

Figure 1.3 Similarities between enterprise computing architectures and open systems standards

How the convergence will affect enterprise computing is yet to be determined. What is likely, however, is that any given organization must:

1. Choose one or both sets of open systems standards, depending on the underlying existing hardware environments.

2. Still utilize integration and interoperability aspects of enterprise computing to bring unsupported hardware and operating systems into the fold of the enterprise under construction.

3. If necessary, still provide hooks and integration between multiple environments within the organization.

Despite the relatively immature nature of many enterprise architectures, there are still many tools and base technologies that can be used to approach and implement enterprise computing. Likewise, there are base technologies and components that can help implement open systems, which, in turn, assist with the achievement of enterprise computing. These are discussed next.

OPERATING SYSTEMS

Most computer professionals associate UNIX with the concept of open systems; some assume that applications developed on top of UNIX are "automatically open," inalienably able to interoperate with one another. Just as there are multiple open systems standards efforts, there are multiple versions of UNIX: AT&T System V, Berkeley BSD (Berkeley Software Distribution), OSF/1, and others.[8] There are various shells and underlying kernels supported by the different variants, and different UNIX versions are the basis for different open systems environments.

Hybrid versions of UNIX have been available for several years (e.g., "UNIX System V with 4.2 BSD extensions"). As the POSIX (discussed next) standards have developed, such hybrid UNIX environments have been taken into account.

POSIX

The "IX" letters in POSIX usually are interpreted as meaning that POSIX is closely related to UNIX, and some may view POSIX as an acronym for "Portable UNIX." In fact, POSIX is an entire family of IEEE standards, not all of which relate directly to operating systems. Let's look at the various POSIX committees and their standards.[9]

1. IEEE 1003.0—Guide to POSIX Open Systems Environments (POSIX.0)—The 1003.0 document functions as an overview of applications portability within the POSIX Open Systems Environment. It helps organizations choose among candidate standards, which is a difficult task given the large number of standards.

2. IEEE 1003.1—System Interface (POSIX.1)—POSIX.1 defines the interface between applications and the operating system in a manner consistent with "historical UNIX." System calls are specified (and eventually will evolve to language-independent instead of C-based).

    Note also that POSIX.1 facilities have been adapted by a number of non-UNIX operating systems. Vendors with proprietary operating systems have added POSIX.1 interfaces in an attempt to move toward opening up their environments. This move toward POSIX.1 should be viewed as very important for enterprise computing environments; basically, developing new applications on top of any POSIX.1-compliant operating system will enhance portability among heterogeneous platforms, even when extensive use is made of local system services.

3. IEEE 1003.2—Shells and Tools (POSIX.2)—Aside from basic services, many of the user interfaces to operating systems are through

tools, shells, scripts, and similar facilities. POSIX.2 is based on the System V shell with additional features inspired by the Korn shell.

4. IEEE 1003.3—Testing and Verification (POSIX.3)—An important aspect to standards and open systems is conformance testing. POSIX.3 is intended to provide a standard methodology for testing conformance of POSIX-based implementations. POSIX.3 is expected to be utilized by organizations such as the Corporation for Open Systems (COS) that offer conformance testing services.

5. IEEE 1003.4—Real-time (POSIX.4)—There are a number of features peculiar to real-time applications, such as timers, semaphores, event management, shared memory, and priority scheduling. As anyone who has ever developed real-time programs knows, such facilities are traditionally handled through system-specific services and routines and have nearly no portability across heterogeneous environments. Adoption of POSIX.4 facilities can be extremely crucial to portability of real-time applications within a heterogeneous enterprise. Instead of requiring extensive rewrites—even with modular code—to port real-time applications to another platform, portability is expected to be relatively straightforward.

6. IEEE 1003.5—Ada Language Bindings (POSIX.5)—Early POSIX working groups were oriented toward C language interfaces to all underlying services. The reliance on a single language, however, is contrary to the very philosophy of open systems for which POSIX is to be used. Therefore, POSIX.5—in conjunction with other groups—defines Ada bindings to the underlying services.

7. IEEE 1003.6—Security Extensions (POSIX.6)—Based on the Department of Defense's "Orange Book," POSIX.6 attempts to standardize security facilities—discretionary access control, mandatory access control, auditing, and privileges—across heterogeneous platforms. Security is a very important aspect to enterprise computing, since the very technical means (interoperability, connectivity) through which enterprise environments are created can inadvertently lead to a great number of security problems. Security is also one of the least standardized areas of computing, which makes "interoperable security" very difficult to achieve without standardization such as POSIX.6.

8. IEEE 1003.7—System Administration (POSIX.7)—Enterprise system management is discussed further in Chapter 2. POSIX.7 is one

means through which heterogeneous systems and network management can be achieved.

9. IEEE 1003.8—Networking (POSIX.8)—POSIX.8 deals with the OSI seven-layer model as well as issues such as transparent file access (1003.8/1—NFS, RFS), protocol-independent network interfaces (1003.8/2—sockets and similar aspects), and remote procedure calls (1003.8/3).

10. IEEE 1003.9—FORTRAN Bindings (POSIX.9)—POSIX.9 performs similar functions for FORTRAN that POSIX.5 does for Ada.

11. IEEE 1003.10—Supercomputing (POSIX.10)—Supercomputing environments are different from those of "traditional UNIX." Just as POSIX.4 defines portable real-time aspects, POSIX.10 does the same for supercomputing and should facilitate incorporation of supercomputers into enterprise environments.

12. IEEE 1003.11—Transaction Processing (POSIX.11)—A great deal of POSIX.4 (real-time) work is included in POSIX.11, given the similar nature of real-time computing and transaction processing. Most Transaction Processing (TP) monitors today are of a proprietary nature, such as IBM's CICS and Digital Equipment's VAX ACMS. "Open TP" is a goal of various UNIX environments, with TP facilities beginning to be found in UNIX-based products. POSIX.11 attempts to standardize such efforts.

POSIX and Enterprise Computing

POSIX provides candidate solutions to different open systems problems within the context of enterprise computing—that is, POSIX.7-compliant facilities may be one of the "open" solutions to heterogeneous systems and network management that are incorporated into an enterprise framework. Most of the open systems profiles—recommended architectures that cover the range of application and system services, such as information management, communications, messaging, and so forth—include some of the various POSIX components as their chosen solutions to different service areas. Keep in mind, however, that many enterprises require additional interoperability facilities for the heterogeneous sub-enterprises that may not readily support the "open solution."

CLIENT/SERVER COMPUTING FOR THE ENTERPRISE

As prevalent as "open systems" and "enterprise computing" have become in terms of corporate strategies, product marketing by vendors, and other areas, most IS professionals would agree that the undisputed champion of the battle for the CHIEF BUZZWORD is: client/server computing

Client/Server Computing

It's difficult to find a product—hardware, systems software, application software, peripheral, communications, or any other—that does not claim support for, implementation of, or other goodness related to client/server computing. The frenzy has accelerated to the point where 1994 was a landmark year in terms of nearly every last holdout jumping on the client/server bandwagon.

In the following sections, we'll focus on the relationship of that computing paradigm with various aspects of enterprise computing. We'll concentrate on the various service areas and architectural aspects of enterprise computing that we discuss in this book and discuss the role of client/server computing in those areas, setting the stage for our discussion in this book.[10]

MOTIVATIONS FOR CLIENT/SERVER COMPUTING

Just as enterprise computing encompasses numerous underlying technologies, client/server computing is based on the following hardware and software aspects:

- desktop systems (personal computers and workstations)
- local area networks (LANs)
- wide area networks (WANs)
- communications interoperability
- graphical user interfaces
- database management systems

The fundamental principles of client/server computing are based around economics and flexibility. Much has been written about the relative costs (both on a total dollar basis and on a "per MIP" basis) of

LAN-based and even WAN-based client/server environments versus traditional centralized corporate mainframes. Even within the realm of client/server models, costs have dramatically decreased in recent years. For example, the typical 64Kb-memory, MS-DOS–based personal computer with a 10- or 20-megabyte hard disk once cost between $2,000 and $3,000; LAN connections typically ran at $300+ per computer. Today—with the free-fall in prices in the past few years—systems with many megabytes of memory, hundreds of megabytes of disk storage, and much faster processors can be found for less than $1,000. Similar decreases in price have occurred with workstations and other hardware components. Economic pressures such as these have given a tremendous cost advantage in the hardware realm to a distributed environment, one which might be best implemented through a client/server model.

It should be understood, though, that there are still substantial costs with respect to the development and management of client/server-based environments (i.e., "client/server" doesn't equate to "free"); many of those costs are in the realm of LAN implementation and management, an area we'll discuss next.

LANs and Client/Server Computing

Most client/server implementations are based around LAN technologies. The ability to connect numerous desktop systems not only with one another but also with midrange and even mainframe systems has brought a new focus to the typical IS environment. Traditionally, IS has been "data center oriented" in that the primary decisions about technologies were made in a centralized fashion. The advent of client/server computing has created a "user-centered" environment in which users demand increased flexibility in their hardware and software components. The required flexibility, however, has increased the need for connectivity and cooperability, and this is usually done (at least initially) over a LAN environment. LAN operating systems typically include support for fundamental client/server operations, such as making a connection and managing lower-level protocols.

DATABASE MANAGEMENT

One of the first areas in which client/server computing was widely used was in database management. Take the following representative SQL query from a relational database environment:

```
SELECT user_id, user_name FROM enterprise_log
 WHERE (user_account_balance < 10000 AND
          user_job_code = 557) ;
```

As shown in Figure 1.4, the traditional centralized environment has communicating applications and users (the latter most likely through terminals) sending SQL commands—which in this environment are little more than a string of bytes at the time of transmission—to the DBMS. Within the DBMS itself, there is typically a compiler or interpreter, which must:

- parse the string of bytes

- verify the syntax of the command

- check the schemas, tables, and columns versus the metadata of the requested database

- send an error message back to the user or application if there is a problem

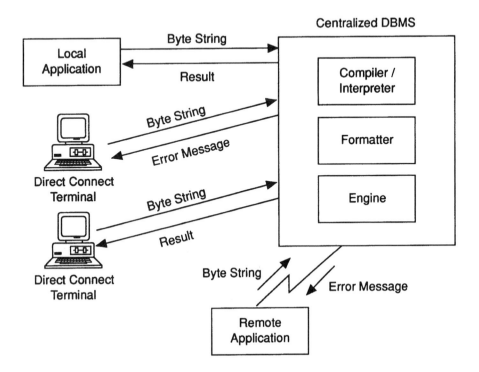

Figure 1.4 Database processing in a traditional environment

- translate the syntax into the appropriate entry point calls for the DBMS engine
- format the resulting data
- transmit the result back to the requestor

There are many inefficiencies with this computing paradigm. Users or applications could flood the DBMS with numerous syntactically invalid SQL statements (bad syntax; referencing invalid columns and/or tables; using an invalid function for a specific data type, such as attempting to do substring manipulation on a column of type INTEGER; and so on). With a centralized environment, the DBMS must be called into play for each and every one of these problem situations, taking valuable processing cycles away from functions such as retrieving data for applications or users who had submitted valid requests.

The retrieved data must be formatted according to some requested display information, which often must be transmitted by the requestor to the DBMS. Even if the DBMS is built around a multithreaded internal architecture, far too many functions are placed on an area that ideally would be better off doing "back-end"—or server—functions.

And that leads us to the alternative architecture, the first place where client/server computing became widely accepted. Figure 1.5 shows a simple DBMS environment built around a client/server architecture; modern DBMS environments can be (and usually are) far more complex.

In this alternative architecture, many tasks, particularly those related primarily to communicating with and validating input from users and applications, reside in a different address space—on some different machine—from that where the back-end, or server, functions exist. Unlike the centralized model, components of the DBMS—the client portions—exist on those separate machines and perform functions such as:

- verify the syntactical correctness of a statement
- translate the request from a string of bytes into a parameterized call to the server's API
- receive data from the server and format it according to the user's requested display or print format

There are still a number of issues that must be resolved within this basic operating framework, and vendors handle some of these functions differ-

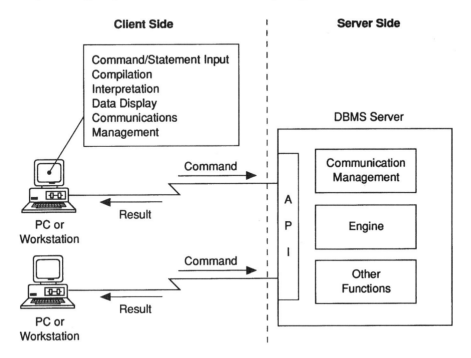

Figure 1.5 Simplified client/server DBMS architecture

ently. For example, suppose a user enters the SQL SELECT statement we showed earlier. If there is a syntax error in the statement, but that problem isn't from, say, misspelling SELECT or reversing the FROM and WHERE clauses but rather from entering an invalid column or table name (say, misspelling "user_id" as "usr_id"), there are several options as to where this error could be caught and reported. In the simplest model, the client portion of the DBMS will verify that the overall syntax of the statement is correct—without validating correct table and column names—and package the statement in the correct API call. The server, upon receipt and the commencement of processing, will detect the misspelling due to the lack of a column known as "usr_id" in the enterprise_log table, and send the appropriate error message back to the client.

The above method still requires both network traffic and server processing for a request that can't be processed due to front-end errors. An alternative method, which requires more functionality of the client side (and this is where we see client components not only of DBMSs but in

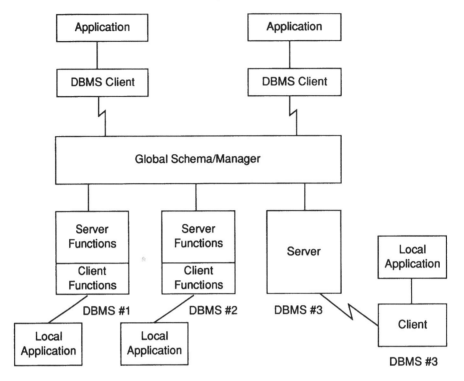

Figure 1.6 Client/server databases within an enterprise

general become more functional than their earlier generations), would have the client:

- fielding the statement from the user or application

- performing the initial syntax validation

- checking the column and table names and definitions against some globally accessible repository, which manages the metadata of the database

- detecting the misspelling before any transmission can be made to the server and reporting the problem to the originating user or application

Let's extend this simple point-to-point model to the larger scope of enterprise computing and see how client/server computing in the database realm functions across an enterprise. Consider the vision of "seamless" access mechanism to heterogeneous stores of information across the enterprise. In framework-based environments the connection between some global interface to the underlying DBMS products can be viewed as a server-based interface. That is, any embedded client functions of the underlying DBMS products are irrelevant to requesting applications and users elsewhere in the enterprise (with the exception, of course, of local applications running against that DBMS without going through a global interface); the only DBMS functions of interest elsewhere are the data stored within their databases and how that information may be retrieved (Figure 1.6).

Applications that can be considered to be "enterprise-based" may communicate with the global schema and manager through client components that likely aren't collocated with any of the DBMS servers or the global manager. This way, a "mix-and-match" approach can be achieved between heterogeneous client and server components as long as the communications protocols are understood and accepted.

USER INTERFACES

It's important to understand that Graphical User Interfaces (GUIs) do not necessarily imply client/server computing; nor do client/server environments always encompass GUIs. Figure 1.7 shows different interface paradigms in both of these areas.

APPLICATION DEVELOPMENT

An important part of any IS environment is the process through which applications are developed. It stands to reason that enterprise-based applications are far more complex than most centralized ones. Additionally, the increased use of servers for most back-end functions introduces additional complexity to the development process.

Let's look at the traditional development model for centralized applications. In a single-platform environment, a common development environment is typically present, one that contains editors, compilers, testing tools, and so forth—all of which are used to develop all components of the application (Figure 1.8).

As client/server computing is introduced to the enterprise, typically in some departmental environment, heterogeneity may become present in the development environment. If, for example, the client systems are MS-DOS and OS/2 PCs while the server is a UNIX workstation, multiple editors, testing tools, and run-time management monitors might suddenly

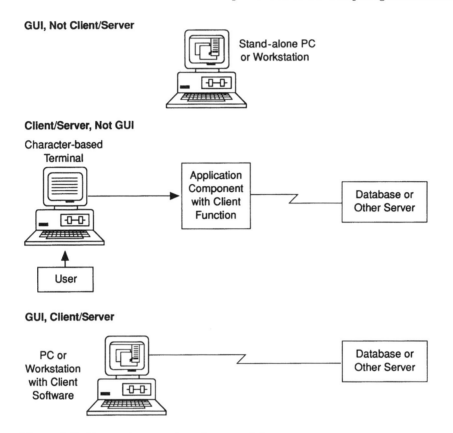

Figure 1.7 Alternative user interface models

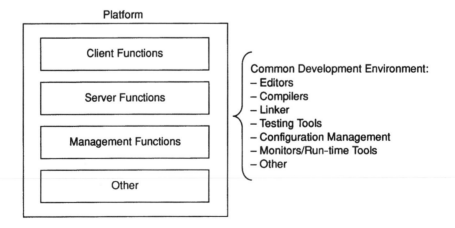

Figure 1.8 Developing centralized applications

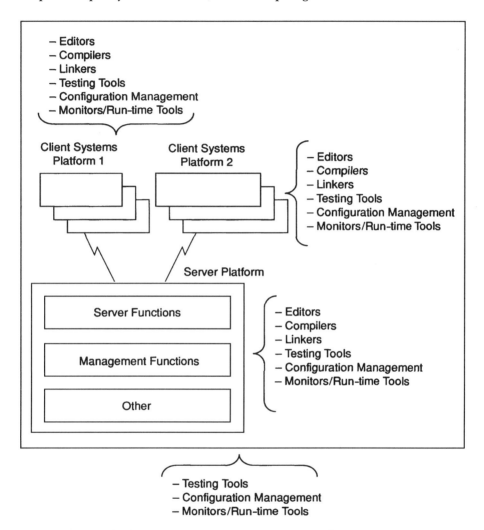

Figure 1.9 Developing departmental client/server applications

become necessary, necessitating an increased level of expertise in the skill base of the developers. Additionally, some tools from the run-time environment may be required to operate on the environment as a whole (e.g., a testing tool for the entire application, not just the client or server portion); these must also be factored into the complexity picture (see Figure 1.9).

Finally, Figure 1.10 shows how application development complexity is increased even more as client/server departmental systems are incorporated into an enterprise computing environment. A standard guideline is

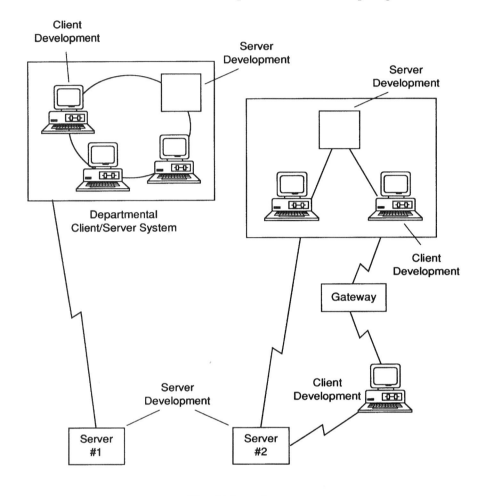

The Enterprise

Figure 1.10 Developing enterprise-wide client/server applications

that the more different hardware and operating system platforms present on both client and server components throughout the enterprise, the more complex the development environment is likely to be (with a preponderance of tools). Even when a development methodology is centered around localized coding on PCs and workstations—using common editors and uploading server code to the respective targets—the configuration management, testing, monitoring, and other functions must still be facilitated on both a component-by-component basis and on a larger scale. These factors should be considered when a development environment is being planned.

On the bright side, however, many of the basic development functions—CASE-based design and development, editor-based coding, source code management, and so on—can be done on client systems, offloading those processing cycles and storage requirements from the mainframes and other servers.

MIDDLEWARE AND NEXT-GENERATION CLIENT/SERVER TECHNOLOGY

The discussion in this chapter about client/server computing and, for that matter, open systems, is principles-oriented, that is, it is aimed at those information technology professionals whose roots are in the centralized mainframe and minicomputer realms and who need to quickly come up to speed with respect to these technologies. In reality, both the open systems and client/server areas—revolutionary in and of themselves—have undergone a great deal of evolution since the early days of each.

One of the areas that is pervasive in both and is arguably the linkage point between open systems and client/server technology in modern applications is the adoption of multiple-level architectures, in which not only are client and server functions separated from one another (as discussed in this chapter) but an additional functionality layer—one "in the middle" between the client and server domains—is part of the information systems landscape. Chapter 2 will discuss this area of middleware in more detail, from the differences between "fat client" and "thin client" computing models to the principles behind middleware technology.

SUMMARY

This first chapter has provided a concise introduction to open systems and client/server computing, setting the stage for our discussion in this book about more advanced forms of client/server architectures and the base technologies required to make those visions reality. The reader is directed to the sources listed in the Endnotes for further information about the subjects discussed in this chapter.

ENDNOTES

1. A. Simon, *Network Re-Engineering: Foundations of Enterprise Computing* (Cambridge, MA: AP Professional, 1994), Chap. 3.

2. A. Simon and T. Wheeler, *Open Systems Handbook,* 2d ed. (Cambridge, MA: AP Professional, 1994).

3. Quoted in K. Patch, "Users Assert Control," *Open Systems Focus,* Summer 1991, p. 8.

4. Ibid.

5. Unsigned article, *Open Systems Focus,* Summer 1991, p. 26.

6. Unsigned research report, "A Plague on 'Open Systems,'" The Gartner Group, June 19, 1991.

7. A. Simon, *Enterprise Computing* (New York: Bantam Books/Intertext, 1992), Chap. 2.

8. Unsigned research report, UniForum, *Your Guide to POSIX,* p. 6.

9. Ibid, pp. 10–15.

10. Material in this section is based on B. Marion, *Client/Server Strategies,* (New York: McGraw-Hill, 1993).

2

Next-Generation
Client/Server
Architectures

INTRODUCTION

It may seem odd that just as client/server technology finally takes hold within production information systems environments—after a number of years of false starts and generally unfulfilled expectations—we discuss the "next generation" of client/server architectures. It is precisely for this reason, though—the general lack of suitability for real-world applications—that this next generation of architectural alternatives and supporting base technologies has emerged and gained a foothold in the information systems world.

In this chapter, we'll discuss a number of architecturally related topics with respect to "modern" client/server technology, beginning with the evolution from the first generation of client/server computing to new technologies designed to overcome the shortcomings of that first generation.

THE FIRST GENERATION: A "C" REPORT CARD

In Chapter 1 we discussed some basic principles of client/server computing, specifically the fundamental principle of establishing a line of demarcation between different portions of an application. The classical approach in the early days of client/server technology was to separate some application back-end functions, specifically those dealing with information management (e.g., the database), from the other functions in the application. Let's look at this in more detail.

In nearly every case, an application has three major components:

- presentation (the portion with which the user interacts)
- business logic (the "thinking portion" of the application)
- data management (the storage and retrieval of data, ideally done in the most expedient manner and always in conjunction with data integrity rules)

All three of these areas communicate with one another—that is, they share data and control information—as shown in Figure 2.1.

Note that, for example, the presentation portion must communicate with the business logic (e.g., some logic must determine what screen to present to the user under what circumstances), the business logic portion must communicate with the data management area (retrieving data as requested by the user from a screen or in conjunction with precoded logic), and so on.

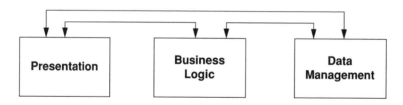

Figure 2.1 Communications among the three major application components: a conceptual view

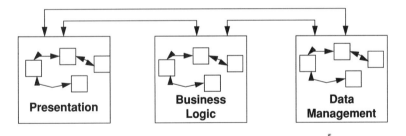

Figure 2.2 Decomposing the communications among application areas

In reality, the conceptual picture of Figure 2.1 is more complex in that each of the three areas is usually made up of a number of subcomponents; that is, a number of modules might exist within the business logic area, and these modules communicate with each other (e.g., one module activating another because of some data condition or in response to the processing logic for a user command), not only within each area but with modules of another area. A more detailed—but still conceptual—illustration of the required communications is shown in Figure 2.2.

Let's now focus on the physicalization—the implementation—of the communications requirements as illustrated above.

Under a centralized processing architecture, such as that shown in Figure 2.3, all three components—and therefore all modules within each component—reside within a single physical computer. Regardless of:

- the complexity of the application (i.e., how many modules exist within each area)

- how structured—or not—the application is (i.e., if it is highly modular with efficient use of subroutines, procedures, and functions, or if, over time, it has evolved to a spaghetti-code form that is difficult to understand)

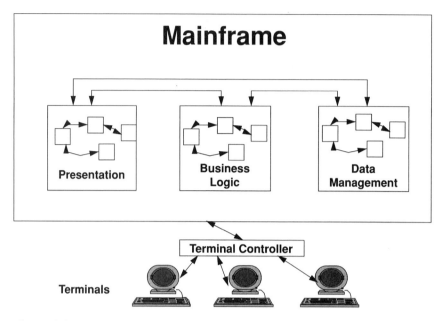

Figure 2.3 Example centralized mainframe-based processing architecture

- what software products are used, whether the code is home-grown (and if so, how it was developed), how many interapplication interactions are part of the environment

. . . and similar factors, the following is true: Because all modules of the three component pieces reside on a single computer, all intermodule exchanges of data and control information are handled within the bounds of that single computer. That is, whether modules communicate with each other by one main program calling a number of subroutines (i.e., a COBOL application paradigm) or via complex multitasking (e.g., Ada tasking, UNIX or VMS interprocess communications, etc.) or by one program invoking one or more entry points of another program, *everything takes place on that computer within the same address space.* Even on older computers that don't feature virtual memory operating systems and require the programmer to manage segmented memory (e.g., Unisys [formerly Sperry Univac] mainframes with multiple instruction and data banks that must be managed by systems programming functions within the application), all of the "lines" shown in the previous figures and in Figure 2.3 take place within that one computer.

For the many reasons discussed in Chapter 1 with respect to the motivations for client/server computing (e.g., economies of scale, attempts to reduce the applications backlog, the rise of desktop computing and net-working, etc.), it soon became desirable among system and application architects to split out some of the functionality away from the single centralized system—whether it was the mainframe, functioning as a back-end server, or a LAN-based server such as a powerful PC or worksta-tion—and put some of the functionality in the user's desktop computing devices, which had come to take the place of standard terminals. Figure 2.4 illustrates the more or less standard architecture that came to repre-sent first-generation client/server computing.

The following items are noteworthy with respect to the representative architecture shown in Figure 2.4.

1. The same three application domains—presentation, business logic, and data management—are still present just as in a centralized architecture; they are simply divided among multiple computers.

2. With respect to the same three domains still being present, so too are the necessary communications among the three domains (i.e.,

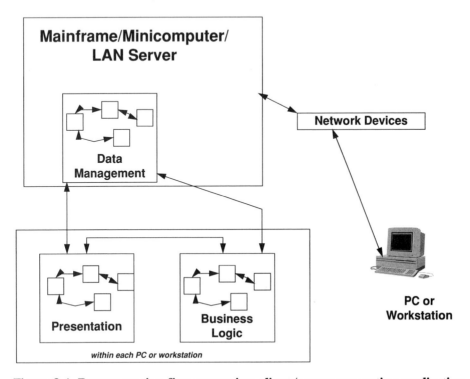

Figure 2.4 Representative first-generation client/server computing application architecture

the presentation portion still needs to communicate with business logic, business logic still needs to communicate with data management, etc.).

3. Finally, with respect to point 2 above, the required exchange of data and control information among "modules" (to use the term generically) that may now be located on different computers requires a more complex communications mechanism than had previously been necessary within a centralized environment. Because, for example, module A within the business logic portion now resides within the desktop computing environment but still needs to communicate with module B of data management, which is on a server, the *network* must now become involved. It is no longer as "simple" as one procedure or function calling another to facilitate the required communications; the very fact that different physical computers have come into play greatly complicates the communications mechanism.

The simple architecture shown in Figure 2.4 shows only a single client desktop computer (though it notes that each client has a similar application architecture of the business logic and presentation components). Consider, however, the more complex architecture shown in Figure 2.5, in which each client has a different component structure than the others in its workgroup (focusing on workgroup, or departmental, computing for now and forgoing larger-scale configurations, such as those crossing the entire enterprise)—that is, some clients may run applications A, B, and C; others run A, B, and D; others run B, D, and E; and so on—and, because of the different component structures, different client applications need to communicate with one another along with one or more servers.

Without going into any level of detail, it is plain to see in Figure 2.5 that the intercomputer communications requirements are far more complex than even those shown in Figure 2.4. This, in turn, implies yet more complications—and deficiencies—with respect to first-generation client/server architectures:

1. The more intercomputer communications are part of an environment, the more "network-literate" the individual modules or groups of modules need to be. Despite attempts to abstract such physicalization away from the modules, there is no getting around

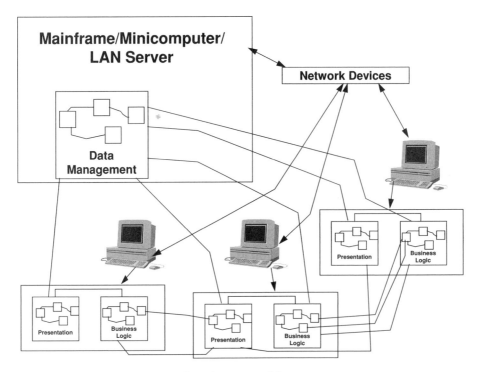

Figure 2.5 A more complex client/server architecture

the fact that a great deal of intercomputer communications and transfer of control and data must occur.

2. In addition to the existence of a great deal of intercomputer communications, there must be some means by which modules that need to communicate with those on another system *know where to go for their needs* (i.e., what physical address on another system, what modules to invoke, and, in general, how to get there). Typically, this directory-oriented information is, under a first-generation client/server architecture, hard-coded into each application component (or, at best, table-driven—stored in tables and loaded at run time).

For all of the above reasons, it is arguable that the first generation of client/server computing was, at best, only a moderate success. Outside of relatively simple departmental applications with homogeneous environments (i.e., all UNIX, or all Windows clients with a NetWare server), it was extremely difficult to develop robust, multiplatform, multiapplication environments without extensive delays, numerous false starts, and a great deal of cost overruns.

Adding to the mix is a final complexity, leading into our discussion of next-generation architectures. In all of the above examples, the business logic component is concentrated within the client computer, leading to a "condition" that became known as the *fat client architecture*. Quite simply, a fat client is one in which not only is a great deal of network-oriented and directory-oriented information (as described above) retained, greatly complicating the portion of the applications that resides on the desktop, but most or all of the business logic of the application is also retained. As noted in Chapter 1, with respect to different types of database applications, this requires not only a greatly increased processing load on the desktop (requiring more powerful—and expensive—client computers than may be cost-effective), but it also presents a maintenance problem with respect to making application logic changes following initial deployment. In large workgroups, it is likely that hundreds or thousands of desktop computers are part of the environment, meaning, for example, that if processing logic that ideally should be stored and managed within the database server is instead put on the client, then all updates need to be propagated to each client system. The same is true for directory information and all other items that involve information about the locations of services that are accessible.

EMERGING CLIENT/SERVER ARCHITECTURES: AN OVERVIEW

To combat the two major deficiencies in first-generation client/server systems—the location of the majority of the business logic within desktop clients and the need to maintain location and directory information on the desktop—pressures mounted from the user community toward all those involved in client/server technology (vendors, consultants, etc.) to develop architectural alternatives to overcome these problems.

One of the first steps was the incorporation of *stored procedure logic* into the data management realm. Figure 2.6 summarizes the differences between first-generation client/server database architectures and those containing stored procedure logic within the server.

By equipping the servers with business logic capabilities through DBMS-managed stored procedures, the servers could function as more

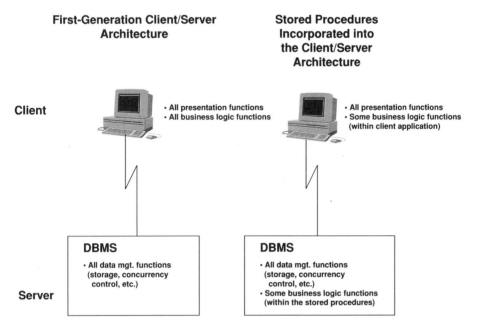

Figure 2.6 Stored procedure-based architectures versus first-generation architectures

than simple data management boxes; now the programming logic of the stored procedures could, for example, call other stored procedures, make determinations as to the success or failure of certain server operations and branch the processing logic accordingly, and perform other tasks, *all without the need for continuous over-the-network direction from the client systems within the environment.*

Even though this movement of business logic represented a major step forward, there were still problems with respect to the other first-generation deficiency—that of the location and directory information (or, to be more precise, the distributed computing services). The need for modules invoking one another across physical computer boundaries did not disappear or even decrease, and, in fact, the placement of some of the business logic functions within the server realm arguably *increased* the need for network-based intermodule exchange of control and data. Additionally, it became more common than in prior situations to have multiple DBMS products, multiple application development environments (i.e., visual development tools), multiple operating environments (Windows, NetWare, UNIX, etc.), and multiple networking protocols (IPX/SPX, TCP/IP, etc.)

. . . all of which complicated the network- and communications-specific information that had to be contained not only within client applications (as before) but now also within the server realm (i.e., one stored procedure communicating with another on a physically separate server). In effect, the application architectures were becoming more complex, with little or no help in the way of commercially available solutions.

This second area of problems—trying to manage the increasingly complex distributed computing services that were part of even departmental and workgroup client/server environments—became fodder for what became known as *middleware*. As discussed in the next section, middleware technology was an attempt to free not only the client applications but also the servers from a great deal of the problems of distributed computing, such as:

- invoking services on another computer
- knowing what computer(s) is available to provide those required services
- managing the flow of data and control according to "business rules"
- managing the transaction semantics across the distributed computing realm (i.e., if a transaction required multiple database servers to be involved, the concurrency control and data integrity functions would be handled not by the local data servers or the client applications but by "something in the middle"—transaction processing middleware)

. . . and so on. Before we move on to further discussion about middleware (more precise definitions, different types of middleware, emerging technologies, etc.), let's first take yet another look at application architectures.

It is a tremendous oversimplification (and also incorrect) to unequivocally state that all first-generation client/server application architectures are "bad" and that the more complex the deployed architecture (i.e., heavy use of stored procedures, extensive middleware, etc.) is, the "better" the environment is. One of the advantages of client/server computing is that because of the smaller scale of the hardware relative to mainframe-based alternatives, nearly any configuration of clients and servers can be constructed. There are, of course, cost issues, support issues (managing distributed systems and LANs, etc.), and other factors that must be considered, but in general the business logic, data management, and presentation portions can be divided in nearly any conceivable manner among the physical computers on a network.

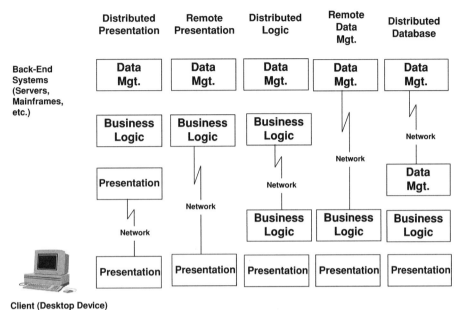

Figure 2.7 Five different client/server architectural alternatives[1]

So what are the determining factors with respect to the configurations and architectures that should be deployed? The answer is "it depends." Factors such as the processes and work flows of the departmental computing applications, what enterprise-wide interoperability must occur, what interoperability *outside* the enterprise must exist (e.g., electronic data interchange with suppliers and customers, Internet-based commercial services, etc.), and numerous other factors must be taken into account. Discussion of these factors with respect to client/server architectures is beyond our scope, but in general there are five different architectural configurations that may be used. These are shown in Figure 2.7. Note that in all five, the same three major components (business logic, data management, and presentation) are part of the architecture; it is the division and allocation of these responsibilities among the clients and servers that make each unique from the other.

Note that the possibilities range from distributed presentation—akin to a centralized processing architecture—and remote data management (first-generation client/server technology) to other alternatives. In general—and, again, this should only be used as a guideline, not a firm rule—*the middle architecture in Figure 2.7, that of distributed logic, is arguably the "architecture of the future."* By allocating *appropriate* application logic to the clients and servers within an environment, the most flexible solutions are likely to be found.

As mentioned above, however, none of these general architectures addresses the problems of distributed computing management; that is, the space in which middleware has grown, as discussed next.

MIDDLEWARE: AN INTRODUCTION

Consider the following relatively simple client/server example, as illustrated in Figure 2.8. Client system A (say, User A's PC) needs to do the following in response to a request from the user:

- access some data from a Sybase database on server system C; based on the data that are retrieved, the client application will either:

    —update other data within that Sybase database server on system C *and* other data within an ORACLE database, the latter residing on server D; or

    —update some data within the ORACLE database on server D and retrieve other data from the same ORACLE database on server D

- depending on which of the above occurs, the client application on A will either:

    —send a message to client system B (if the first option is the case); or

    —send a message to client system E along with the data retrieved from ORACLE database server D, if the second option is the case

With respect to the distributed computing portions (i.e., "making things happen" across physical boundaries), the following tasks must be accomplished:

1. The client application on A must be aware that the data required to support the requested user operation reside on server C, are in a Sybase database, and are accessed over a given network protocol (say, TCP/IP).

2. The client application on A must, after retrieving the requested data, also know that in one case it must return to C to update other data *and*, as part of that same modification transaction, update data on D. With respect to this dual-site update operation, the fact that

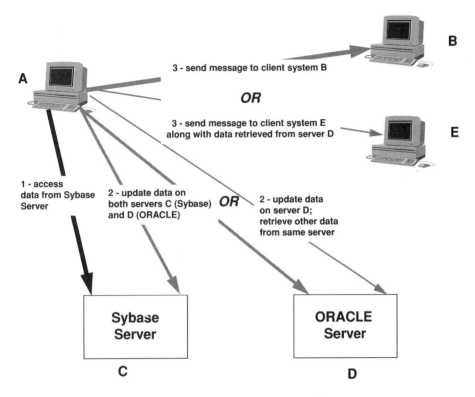

Figure 2.8 Sample client/server data and control flow

there are two different DBMSs means that it is likely that slightly different SQL dialects are used (i.e., different command syntax, different status codes returned to the client, etc.).

3. With respect to the above, there must be *distributed* transaction management, not only across databases but across DBMS products; that is, the all-or-nothing property of database transactions (to maintain data integrity) cannot be handled by a single DBMS instance but rather must be coordinated across both DBMS products and their databases. If, for example, the Sybase update on server C is successful but the ORACLE update on server D is not, some coordinating authority must handle this situation accordingly (i.e., back out the entire distributed heterogeneous transaction, or queue the failed portion of the overall transaction for retry or whatever other protocol is in place).

4. The client application on A must determine to which other client—B or E—a message should be sent, and whatever messaging protocol is in effect (custom, X.400, etc.) for each must be known and used.

. . . and so on. Each of the above distributed computing functions could, in the traditional manner, be handled within either the client or server applications (in the above scenario, the client application running on system A would shoulder the brunt of this responsibility).

Alternatively, the majority of these distributed computing functions could be pushed "into the middle" between the client and server domains within the environment . . . hence the term "middleware."

Though definitions abound for the term "middleware" (just like client/server, open systems, enterprise computing, object-oriented, etc.), a generally accepted and comprehensive definition is the following: *Middleware is the collection of distributed computing services that, within any given processing environment, enables clients and servers to communicate and interoperate with one another in the most expedient, flexible, and correct manner possible.*

For example, the distributed transaction processing requirement of the scenario above—specifically, ensuring that two different DBMSs running on physically separate machines cooperate with one another to guarantee environment-wide data integrity—is *not* a function that should be handled by the client application running on system A. Given the trend away from "fat clients" toward "thin clients" (i.e., client systems with as much processing as possible relocated to other computers), forcing the application and the computer to manage not only this specific distributed transaction in the example but a number of others is a step in the wrong direction with respect to client/server architectures.

Nor is it advisable to force the servers to handle such functionality. While some DBMS products have distributed transaction management capabilities built into their server engines, these typically are homogeneous in nature (e.g., they manage multiple databases running under that DBMS product on different sites) and aren't equipped to handle complex transactions involving other products. Even those DBMS products that offer gateways to other DBMSs (and most will do so by the mid-1990s) typically function in a "relaxed transaction" manner, that is, real-time distributed transactions aren't supported (though many are trending in that direction). The database servers should be left to perform the services they do best and most efficiently—manage local databases.

Since neither the client nor server domains are appropriate for such distributed transaction processing capabilities, that leaves the middle—more specifically, the middleware layer—in which this can and should be done. The middleware layer has evolved to the most appropriate place for functionality, such as:

- distributed transaction processing (as discussed above)

- directory services (i.e., finding out where some required service might be procured)

- abstraction services (i.e., hiding the details of a specific DBMS product from the client application, permitting clients to be architected to work with more than one DBMS without having to hard-code or dynamically construct a large number of DBMS SQL dialects)

- messaging services—enabling clients and servers to communicate with one another in a reliable manner, even when sites aren't immediately available

- interapplication interoperability services—enabling an application running on one system to invoke functionality (i.e., a remote procedure) on another

- work-flow services—based on factors such as the results of some query, timer, externally created situation, and so on, data and control can be automatically routed to the appropriate user, application, or service for timely processing

These and other services can be accessed by clients and servers as necessary in any given environment, in effect pushing many of the requests and interoperability formerly located on one machine—but now distributed—away from the client and server domains.

Conceptually, this seems relatively straightforward. In reality, middleware is far more complex—and several different variations exist—as discussed in Chapter 3.

SUMMARY

In this chapter, we looked at how client/server computing has evolved from a "just put the things on different computers and make them talk" approach, which was often haphazard and architecturally inflexible, into a suite of architectural alternatives that can be tailored according to the needs of any given environment. We also took an introductory look at middleware technology—the set of services that enables the architectural flexibility of next-generation client/server computing to be a reality. In the next chapter, we'll take a more detailed look at middleware, discussing the various alternatives and technologies.

ENDNOTES

1. Adapted from a Gartner Group–provided figure in S. Rabin, "Critical Technical Issues When Building Enterprise Client/Server Applications," *American Programmer*, November 1994, p. 18.

3

Principles of Middleware

INTRODUCTION

In the previous chapter, we defined middleware as the collection of distributed computing services that, within any given processing environment, enables clients and servers to communicate and interoperate with one another in the most expedient, flexible, and correct manner possible. In this chapter, we'll dig deeper into the subject, focusing on the enabling models and underlying technologies for middleware, including:

- the different classes of middleware and the distinctions between each group
- detailed discussions of the underlying technologies and trends within each class
- the future directions of middleware, with respect to general technology and standards

CLASSES OF MIDDLEWARE

As is often the case with emerging computing technologies, there is rarely a clear, distinct categorization of middleware; that is, there are several different classifications, which may be used to divide different middleware

39

technologies into separate groups, and these classifications overlap one another. In this section, we'll briefly look at these various distinctions in preparation for our discussion in subsequent sections.

Database

As with client/server computing in general, the first area in which middleware became widely used was in the area of database management. Within database management, the first functions of middleware were to provide some degree of abstraction from underlying local data managers to client applications, for two purposes:

1. Gateways to other DBMS products—gateway-oriented middleware is used to permit an application that "normally" would run against, for example, a Sybase database to access data that are contained under the management of another DBMS product (e.g., ORACLE or DB2).

2. Multiple-DBMS access—expanding on gateway-oriented middleware, this class of database middleware provides standardized access to multiple underlying DBMS products, handling the various mappings and other interface functions in this layer rather than forcing the client application to do so.

Figure 3.1 illustrates the above two types of database middleware.

As discussed later in this chapter, there are other types of database middleware, such as those used for the management of location and directory-oriented information (i.e., "Where can I find the required data?") and replication (duplicates of data, the synchronization and update policies, etc.).

Peer-to-Peer

Another class of middleware can be termed *peer-to-peer* middleware,[1] which does not have to involve client applications and database servers but rather can be used for:

- clients communicating among themselves (e.g., an application running on one client invoking an application running on another client)

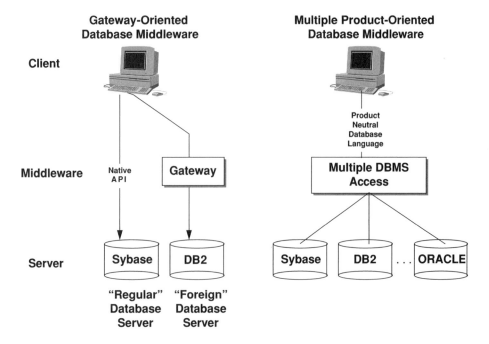

Figure 3.1 Two types of database middleware

- servers communicating among themselves (e.g., a stored procedure running on one database server requesting data from a stored procedure running on another)

- clients or servers communicating with some middleware service (e.g., requesting directory information for an electronic mail application)

As discussed later, these types of interactions can be handled in one of several ways. For purposes of the taxonomy in this section, the distinguishing characteristics of database middleware are that the functions don't necessarily have to be database-oriented, and the interaction does not necessarily have to involve a client application and a database server.

Object-Oriented

Still another categorization that overlaps those above is the distinction between object-oriented middleware and non–object-oriented middleware. As discussed later, the underlying mechanisms (the implementation) of object-oriented middleware could, in fact, be either messaging- or

RPC-based, but for our purposes we'll categorize object-oriented middleware as a different category because applications interact with it differently than with traditional RPC or messaging implementations, which tend to be procedural in nature.

Classifications

Figure 3.2 illustrates one means by which middleware can be categorized. Note that in articles discussing middleware, it is common, as discussed above, to make distinctions between different classes of middleware, but rarely is the same taxonomy used. Instead, the lines of demarcation tend to be drawn differently in one article versus another, such as database versus non-database (peer-to-peer) or RPC versus messaging versus object-oriented. The diagram in Figure 3.2 illustrates that any given middleware component can be categorized in more than one way (e.g., RPC-based and database-oriented; non-database, peer-to-peer, and messaging-oriented; etc.). Note that the lines of demarcation are even a bit fuzzier, since, as mentioned above, and as discussed later, the *interface* paradigm may be different from the actual underlying implementation. For example, object-oriented middleware has, by definition, an object-oriented interface, but the physical underlying means could be built on a messaging scheme. Alternatively, work is being done to provide logical messaging on top of physical RPC interfaces.

The reason the above taxonomy is presented is not so much that a firm distinction can be made among these various classes, but rather to guide

	Messaging	RPC	O-O
Database			
Peer-to-Peer			

Figure 3.2 A taxonomy of middleware classes

the reader through often confusing distinctions made in the swarm of articles and vendor material that often take a slightly different focus from one another with respect to distinguishing among the alternatives available to the user. What is more important is understanding the various uses and tradeoffs among each distinct type of middleware, as discussed in the following sections.

DATABASE MIDDLEWARE

Roots

Two major technological trends of the 1980s—desktop computing (PCs, workstations) and minicomputer-based departmental computing (typically on Digital Equipment VAX and IBM AS/400, but also on midrange systems of Data General and other vendors)—brought to light several problems with respect to organizational data environments. Specifically, applications running on one platform needed access to data running on

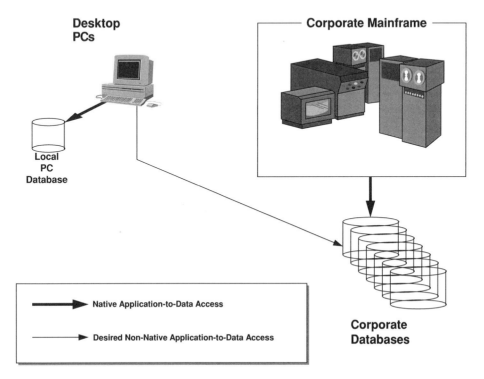

Figure 3.3 Desired cross-platform data access

another platform, *which typically was of a different hardware and operating systems variety.* Figure 3.3 illustrates a typical access "wish list" of this variety.

For much of the 1980s, it was expected that the eventual advent of distributed database technology would provide the primary solution to the above access problem. Specifically, the distributed database management system (DDBMS) would provide the services and facilities through which applications could run against a "global schema" and both *location* and *format* of data would be abstracted away from the applications. Figure 3.4 illustrates the representative structure of a DDBMS environment.

As of the mid-1990s, DDBMS technology has been rarely deployed outside of specialized situations, in effect removing this architectural approach as a candidate solution to the heterogeneous data access problem. There are a number of reasons for this lack of acceptance, such as immature technology, performance problems, and management issues.[2]

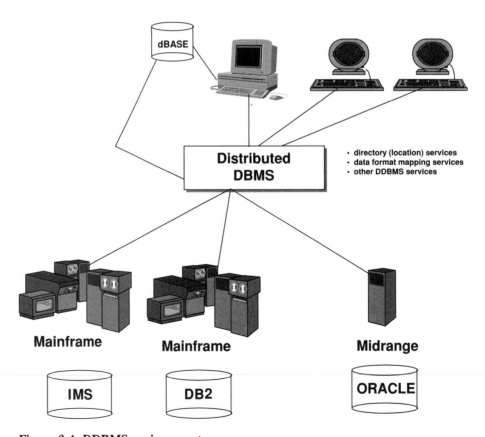

Figure 3.4 DDBMS environment

To fill the void in this realm, products that provided some degree of heterogeneous data access, although not the full complement of DDBMS functions (location transparency, distributed transaction management, etc.), appeared. *In effect, the first generation of database middleware materialized.*

As the 1980s moved forward, a number of external trends, specifically those related to corporate mergers and acquisitions, fueled the need for database middleware access services. As companies acquired one another, there suddenly was a tremendous need for a VAX-based accounting application to be able to access accounting data from the mainframe, for customer and client lists to be merged even though they resided on several different platforms, and so on. This provided even more impetus for database middleware usage.

Next Steps

Over time, heterogeneous database access became somewhat of a commodity. Though facilities would vary from one product to another, the cross-platform boundaries no longer prevented access to data needed by an application, even if that information was located on a foreign platform. This access was prompted by standardization efforts built exclusively around heterogeneous database access, such as the SQL Access Group's (SAG's) efforts, which gave rise to Microsoft Corporation's Open Database Connectivity (ODBC) effort.[3]

Simple access, though, is not sufficient for many applications. As the scope covered by an architecture grew from simple departmental LANs to the enterprise, the need arose for many additional services to augment those found in the access.

One of these service areas is that of database replication . . . the *controlled* duplication of selected portions of information across multiple physical platforms. Ironically, one of the primary motivations of distributed database technology was to eliminate as much data duplication as possible; by using the DDBMS facilities, application and user requests would automatically be directed to *the* source of the required data. While vendors were working on DDBMS technology, they provided simplistic replication capabilities as sort of a "stopgap" measure until the "real" DDBMS facilities arrived.

As DDBMS technology sputtered and stalled, those leading-edge implementors took a look at the replication capabilities they had and drew up strategic plans and architectural alternatives based around replication rather than distributed database capabilities. Surprisingly, the deficiencies inherent in replication weren't as serious as had been held by conventional wisdom, but the architectural and data management constraints imposed by distributed database technology turned out to be more serious than had been envisioned. In effect, the stopgap measure of distributed data management—replication—gained so much acceptance that many DBMS vendors shifted their efforts away from their DDBMS plans to enhancing replication facilities.

It is through the paradigm shift from DDBMS to replication that database middleware began to grow past simple heterogeneous access into more functional, robust sets of capabilities. Replication management middleware began to appear in the mid-1990s. It's important to note that a variety of different replication mechanisms are available, and the effectiveness of each will vary according to factors such as the major usage of the environment and the particulars of any organization's architecture. For example, some replication models are more suited to decision support systems (DSSs) and executive information systems (EISs), specifically

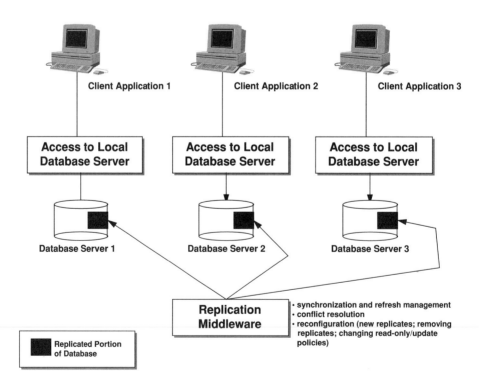

Figure 3.5 Middleware-based replication

for "stocking" data warehouses, or informational databases (as opposed to transactional, or operational, databases).[4] Other models are more useful for replication of transaction processing databases, that is, those databases supporting high-volume, high-throughput environments.

Regardless of specifics of any particular replication implementation, what *is* consistent across the multiple models is the need for middleware services to accomplish and manage the replication. That is, just as in any of the "standard" client/server models discussed in Chapter 2, in which necessary services (i.e., database language translation) are located in neither the client nor the server but rather in between, the functions necessary for replication support would likewise be located and managed by middleware-based software. Figure 3.5 presents a simple illustration of middleware-based replication.

A variation of the above theme that is also gaining popularity is the use of replication to support a data warehouse (i.e., informational database) environment. Figure 3.6 illustrates how replication-enabled middleware can extract pertinent data from operational databases, perform the necessary summarizations and structural modifications, and "stock" the ware-

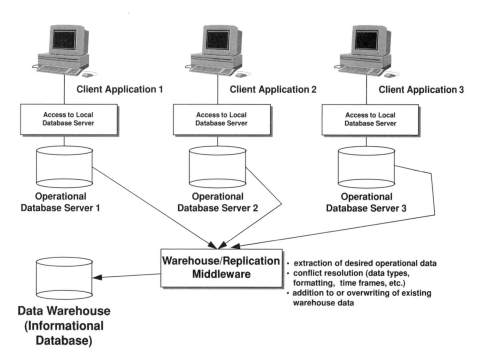

Figure 3.6 Replication middleware used for data warehouse management

house in accordance with the policies of the organization (i.e., at some given frequency).

Location Transparency

Another class of database-oriented middleware is that used to provide some degree of *location transparency*. That is, rather than hard-coding into all client applications all network addresses of the locations of database services and, more precisely, which services can provide what specific data, directory-oriented middleware can be used for dynamic lookups and run-time determination of such location information. The roots of location transparency are in the DDBMS world, and, even as DDBMS technology has fallen out of favor, some degree of location transparency remains important to *some* classes of applications. At present (mid-1990s), a *general* demarcation is that location transparency is unsuitable for transaction processing applications (again, high throughput requirements) because of the increased processing overhead and performance impediments introduced by the run-time location determination. However, other appli-

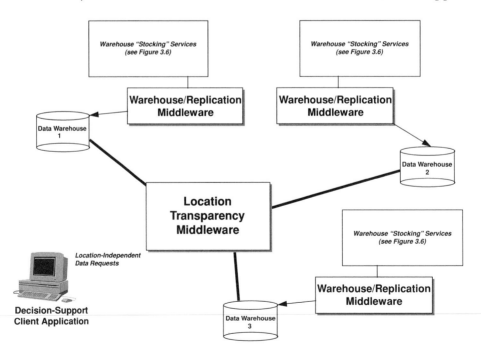

Figure 3.7 Location transparency middleware

cation classes, particularly those oriented toward decision support, which are "discovery-oriented" (e.g., "search for 'interesting' data *anywhere* in the enterprise") with unpredictable, ad hoc queries, rather than driven by rigid performance constraints (e.g., an absolute requirement to process *n* transactions per second), are suitable for location transparency services. Very often these location transparency services are used within the data warehouse realm, as illustrated in Figure 3.7.

RPC MIDDLEWARE

As application architectures become increasingly complex, the need for middleware has expanded beyond that of the database-oriented mechanisms described above. Specifically, the concept of *application partitioning*, in which formerly singular applications are decomposed and placed on multiple platforms, requires that the components be able to invoke one another and share control information and data as necessary (as was discussed earlier).

While cross-platform application communication is complex enough in homogeneous (e.g., only one variety of hardware and operating system) environments, it becomes more difficult when heterogeneity is added to the picture. One early mechanism, which is still widely used, is that of *remote procedure calls* (RPCs). As implied by the name, the RPC mechanism uses a procedure call paradigm as would be found within a single-platform program structure, but extends it into the network realm, enabling procedure calls to be made from one computer to another.

Traditionally RPC facilities have been synchronous, that is, one procedure calls another and waits for the response to come back before proceeding (Figure 3.8).

The calling application is "blocked," that is, it waits for the result (or error condition or some other return status) to be returned from the remote procedure before proceeding.

RPC mechanisms may be used in any type of distributed computing environment between any two components (i.e., a client to a server, one client to another, one server to another, from one middleware component to another, etc.). Multiple RPCs may be "strung together," that is, a client application can call another, which in turn calls a server procedure to obtain data that are to be returned to the original requestor.

One of the purported shortcomings of RPC models is that the synchronous nature can cause bottlenecks and performance problems in environ-

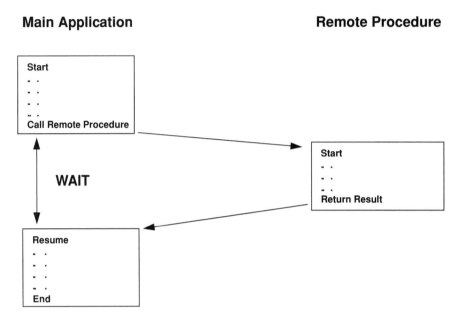

Figure 3.8 RPC synchronization operation

ments other than relatively small LANs with one or two servers . . . and a homogeneous network and systems software infrastructure (i.e., all UNIX and TCP/IP).[5] To overcome these claimed deficiencies, a new class of middleware has evolved in recent years and appears to be passing RPC models in terms of usage in complex heterogeneous client/server environments. This middleware class—messaging—is discussed next.

MESSAGING MIDDLEWARE

Unlike RPC technology, messaging middleware is inherently asynchronous. Built around the passing of messages, each component of an application (client, server, middleware services) can make its own determination as to whether or not processing should continue while waiting for a response to its message, and, if so, what exactly should be done.

Conceptually, message-oriented middleware (MOM) is relatively simple to understand and, in fact, is very much like building applications around electronic mail. Applications send messages to other applications (or components thereof) by placing messages into one or more queues, typically organized around the types of services needed. A local queue manager then determines if the request can be satisfied locally or if a remote service needs to be used, and the message is passed to that remote service.[6] Meanwhile, the requesting application can pursue other processing (determined by the application logic) until a response comes back via the queue manager.

As with the other topics in this chapter, messaging can be handled in a point-to-point manner (i.e., from one client application directly to another, from a client application to a server, etc.), or a middleware component can be added to the architecture. In effect, once the local queue manager determines that it is necessary to pass the message to an outside service, the message can be given to middleware for determination as to the destination instead of hard-coding the distributed message control within the application itself. This model is very similar to that of an *object broker*, a technology used in object-oriented middleware (discussed next). The message middleware acts as a "broker," determining for any given message and its particular attributes what the most appropriate destination of that message should be.

The asynchronous nature of message-oriented middleware arguably gives this paradigm an edge over RPC technology in complex, large-scale environments, particularly those that are heterogeneous. To support this complexity and heterogeneity, the Message-Oriented Middleware Association (MOMA), a consortium of vendors with the charter to "promote MOM technology and educate potential customers about the technology's benefits through seminars, developer conferences, and other marketing activities," was formed in 1994.[7] The goal of MOMA, at least as of the time of writing, is not to become another standards organization but rather to promote interoperability across vendors' product lines and to develop standard terminology.[8] Many efforts by MOMA vendors are dedicated to closing the gap between RPC and MOM technologies and practices, in effect bringing about a coexistence of these two middleware approaches and alleviating the either/or nature faced by systems architects today.

OBJECT-ORIENTED MIDDLEWARE

In the previous section, it was mentioned that message-oriented middleware is conceptually similar to that of object brokers. In effect, emerging object paradigms are used across a distributed computing environment. One model is Microsoft's Common Object Model (COM), the basis for

Object Linking and Embedding (OLE). A competing model—the System Object Model (SOM)—is the basis for the Common Object Request Broker Architecture (CORBA) and OpenDoc strategy, proposed by other vendors such as IBM and Apple.[9]

When object-oriented middleware is used, a set of services is used to route requests to the appropriate object method and to route results back to the requestor . . . much as message-oriented middleware operates. The primary distinction is the object-oriented nature of the applications as opposed to more traditional applications (i.e., those that are procedural in nature).

FUTURE DIRECTIONS

The middleware area is evolving so rapidly that a conscious decision was made with respect to this book to avoid technical details that could become obsolete rather quickly. For example, during the writing of this book, the Message-Oriented Middleware Association (MOMA) was formed, changing the complexion of standardization in that realm. The COM-versus-SOM wars continue as new alliances form and cross-vendor strategies change along with buyouts and corporate restructurings.

It's far more valuable to look at some of the larger trends in the middleware area, including the following:

- Database Middleware: Replication and data warehousing continue to be the fastest growing areas, and it's expected that by the late 1990s this area will achieve phenomenal growth and far more pervasive usage than today's mostly experimental implementations. To support these approaches to distributed data management, ever more robust middleware facilities will come to market.

- RPC Technology: The convergence of MOM and RPC technologies will likely put an end to the either/or decision process facing architects today. Additionally, it is expected that 1995 will be the year in which the Distributed Computing Environment (DCE) "comes into its own," transitioning out of pilot programs on relatively small departmental systems into larger-scale, full-production environments.

- Message-Oriented Middleware: Primarily due to the growth of MOMA, MOM technology will likely evolve to be the predominant cross-component interoperability paradigm within the procedural application world (i.e., as opposed to object-oriented applications).

- Object-Oriented Middleware: Conventional thought holds that since the multivendor SOM is a superset of Microsoft's COM, these two approaches will eventually converge, leading to cross-platform object services that span from the Windows desktops (where COM, via OLE, is dominant) to midrange and larger mainframe systems (where CORBA facilities represent the preeminent object models).

SUMMARY

In this chapter we looked at middleware from the viewpoint of being the enabling technology for flexible distributed computing. Regardless of the specific class of middleware (database, peer-to-peer, object-oriented) or the specific mechanism (i.e., message-oriented or RPC), the principles of middleware are simply to enable clients and servers to communicate and interoperate with one another in the most expedient, flexible, and correct manner possible. Like other "hot" areas of computing, middleware will continue to evolve, and it is *strongly* recommended that client/server and distributed computing architects, strategic planners, and other decision-makers stay abreast of advances in these realms to the greatest extent possible.

ENDNOTES

1. This term is used in P. Korzeniowski, "With C/S Apps, Middle Can Become Bottom Line," *Software Magazine,* July 1994, pp. 59–60, to refer to both remote procedure call (RPC) and messaging middleware.

2. This is discussed further in A. Simon, *Strategic Database Technology: Management for the Year 2000* (San Mateo, CA: Morgan Kaufmann, 1995), Chaps. 2–7.

3. Ibid., Chap. 3.

4. Data warehouses and replication are discussed in detail in ibid., Chaps. 4–5. Further information about different replication models may be found in G. Schussel, "Database Replication: Playing Both Ends against the Middleware," *Client/Server Today,* November 1994, pp. 57–67.

5. C. Amaru, "Building Distributed Applications with MOM (Message-Oriented Middleware)," *Client/Server Today,* November 1994, p. 85.

6. R. Whiting, "Getting on the Middleware Express," *Client/Server Today*, November 1994, p. 74.

7. Ibid.

8. Ibid.

9. T. Lewis and M. Evangelist, "Fat Servers versus Fat Clients: The Transition from Client/Server to Distributed Computing," *American Programmer*, November 1994, p. 8.

PART II

Case Study 1

4

Overview of ProtoGen+

INTRODUCTION

The ProtoGen+ Workbench is an integrated environment of tools, bringing together the resources and components necessary to construct Microsoft Windows–based applications. It integrates a series of code generation tools that can be used to output source code in one of several target programming languages, including:

- ANSI C
- C++ for Borland's Object Windows Library
- C++ for Microsoft's Foundation Class Library
- Pascal code for Borland's Pascal with Objects

The ProtoGen+ Workbench integrates text editors, font editors, icon editors, and bitmap editors for further manipulation and control of the resources needed in GUI applications. Programmers have easy access to the source code that is generated and included with the application, functioning in a visual development mode.

Within Windows environments, Dynamic Link Libraries (DLLs) are an important part of application development. Windows DLLs replace the use of conventional DOS object libraries, which required static linkage to the program executable (and the loading of the entire module into memory when the program was run). In Windows, dynamic linking eliminates the need to have all code present in memory at once. ProtoGen+, like Windows itself, consists of a dynamic link library (PVPLUS.DLL), which provides a set of functions to simplify and ease the development of complex applications. In some cases, ProtoGen+ functions replace standard Windows functions because a higher level of functionality is needed; in other cases, completely new functions are provided for the application developers.

PROTOGEN+ COMPONENTS

As was mentioned above, ProtoGen+ contains a number of products and libraries to provide visual development services to programmers. These include ViewPaint, SQLView, the Menu Designer, and the ProtoView libraries. Each is briefly discussed below and in more detail in the following chapters. The ProtoGen+ Workbench might be viewed as the "master control center" or hub of the ProtoGen+ application development environment. From the Workbench each of the above-mentioned tools can be accessed, along with code generation modules and other text and resource editors. Further—arguably most importantly, to some developers—compilation, testing, and execution can be accomplished from the Workbench. 3GL programmers who are used to batch compiles and time-consuming testing and problem analysis are usually especially appreciative of facilities such as this.

The Menu Designer

The Menu Designer utility permits the developer to create menu resources and save them to menu template files (with a .MNU extension). Each .MNU file contains a menu resource that may be edited and reused.

The Menu Designer supports predefined menu pop-up templates for the standard FILE, EDIT, MDI WINDOWS, and HELP. Templates make it easy to quickly build a standard menu for applications. The developer can also define his or her own menu pop-up templates in files with a .MTP extension.

The Menu Designer permits cascaded menus with grayed and checked items to be built, along with accelerator keys and menu breaks. Cut-and-paste operations between various submenus can also be performed. Dynamic status messages can be entered and associated with any menu item;

these are then displayed in the application's status line whenever the menu item is selected. Finally, bitmaps can be specified as menu items and displayed as the menu is designed. The bitmap resources are added to the application and loaded automatically at run time.

ViewPaint

ViewPaint permits the developer to design and edit dialog resource files. Dialog boxes and data entry screens may be "painted" in a What You See Is What You Get (WYSIWYG) manner with custom colors, field editing, error messages, and automatic OK/CANCEL processing. Variable names and window function names can be specified for any and all fields. As screens are painted, detailed editing criteria can be specified, and specific error messages can be created and specified.

Data validation criteria may be established through ViewPaint for controls on the dialog screen. These criteria include range checking, choice checking, table lookups, and mandatory fields. ViewPaint's Test Mode permits the experimentation of the application (i.e., test runs) with error message display and live table lookups.

Text and background colors can be selected from a palette of predefined colors; alternatively, custom colors can be created using slider controls. These custom colors can be specified for an entire view or for individual field controls. Font and type styles (e.g., boldface, underlined, italicized, etc.) can also be specified.

Field method strings are used to associate data with ProtoGen+ objects. The ProtoGen+ objects then use those data to control their behavior. For example, a field method string might contain some error message, a list of valid inputs, provide a bitmap file name, generate a beep, or supply other data to a control. These are used to provide functionality without coding; the point and click interface permits the user to attach field method strings to the entire view or selected fields. These are similar to the use of properties in Visual BASIC controls.

ViewPaint also permits the developer to design and select toolbars that will automatically be loaded and displayed on the top, bottom, and either side of any data entry form or dialog box. The toolbars act like child windows of a view and are automatically positioned and sized to give the user access to commonly used application functions.

Error messages and help messages can be created through ViewPaint. Additionally, Dynamic Data Exchange (DDE) links can be established and tested through the ProtoGen+ Workbench ViewPaint. A DDE "conversation" is automatically set up and managed while the dialog is being designed; this is accomplished by entering an application name, topic, and optional item name for both a server field and a client field. The DDE links are live in ViewPaint Test Mode, so they can be experimented with.

ViewPaint is also used to access any of the ProtoGen+ code generators. A generated application can be compiled, linked, executed, and debugged.

The ProtoView Screen Manager

The ProtoView Screen Manager acts as a functional layer between Microsoft Windows and application programming, performing tasks and managing data on behalf of the application program. It replaces the standard Windows Dialog Manager. It contains a function library—a DLL—with approximately 175 screen management functions to control the appearance and behavior of screens. The ProtoView Screen Manager offloads many of the user interface functions from the overall application (see the discussion in Part I about the structure of client/server applications), permitting the application/business logic to be the "primary" focus of application developers rather than the mundane details of Windows screen management.

Data conversion from application variables to on-screen text and back is also handled, along with colors, Multiple Document Interface (MDI) screens, and dynamic status lines.

Other Libraries

Other ProtoGen+ libraries include the WinControl control library, an expandable DLL of Windows custom controls. Each control is capable of handling user input in a predefined and uniform manner without application assistance. ProtoGen+ ensures that if an application specifies a variable to be associated with a field, all updates are handled as necessary. Additionally, a "subclassing" capability permits developers to change an aspect of a field's characteristics (i.e., behavior or appearance) as required by a given application. A set of utility functions for text drawing, field editing, mouse processing, and DDE message handling is also included in the WinControl control library.

SQLView is used to provide visual database access. Note with respect to the discussion in Part I the demarcation between the user interface, application/business logic, and data management realms. In the ProtoGen+

environment, ProtoGen+ itself and the ProtoView Screen Manager are concerned primarily with the front-end, UI-oriented services and components. SQLView is used to provide database and back-end services. SQLView services can be used to access any database that supports an Open Database Connectivity (ODBC) database driver or the Q+E Database Library. Using SQLView along with ProtoGen+ enables both the client and database server sides to be visually developed.

In addition to the various code generators of the ProtoGen+ environment, there is an interface to Visual Coders, a set of modules that can be modified and installed to implement code generation for specific types of functionality. Examples include Common Dialog Visual Coders, Multi-Media, OLE, MAPI, and others.

GENERAL WORKBENCH FEATURES

The ProtoGen+ Workbench permits developers to link dialog resources and data entry screens to menu items and pushbutton objects on other dialogs. New dialog resources can be created and existing forms edited from directly within the Workbench itself. Dialogs and data entry forms are often the primary building blocks of an application, since they are the components with which the user interacts.

Functionality may be attached at many different points in applications . . . to pushbuttons, menu items, bitmaps, and icons. ProtoGen+ refers to these components as *functional points*. These are the most common and intuitive screen objects used to attach functionality and add processing to an application. The ProtoGen+ Workbench supports seven standard types of functionality that can be attached to any functional point. These are:

1. Dialog box resources

2. MDI dialog resources

3. MDI child windows

4. Pop-up windows

5. Program executables

6. User-defined functionality (i.e., visual coders)

7. Function code

These are briefly discussed below.

Dialog Boxes and Data Entry Screens

These are user-interface elements created with ViewPaint (discussed above) and saved to a disk file. Data entry screens are similar to dialog boxes except that they serve specifically as the vehicle through which application users enter data, thus playing an important role in the substance of an application. They are usually displayed for a longer period of time than "standard" dialog boxes, and the data returned from them (i.e., the user's entries) are more critical to the application's central function than responses to simple dialog-based controls.

MDI Dialogs

ProtoGen+ MDI dialogs conform to Microsoft specifications for applications that use multiple copies of a similar type of user window (e.g., a word processing package editing multiple files or a drawing package editing multiple diagrams). Each window can be tiled or cascaded along with other editing windows. ProtoGen+ extends this principle to the use of data entry screens in business applications where multiple copies of a single data entry form may be needed by a user (i.e., working on entering multiple records at once). MDI dialogs in ProtoGen+ behave the same as any other MDI windows; the only difference is that the contents of Proto-Gen+ MDI dialogs can be read from application resources. The Proto-Gen+ Workbench permits developers to attach ProtoGen+ MDI dialogs as functional points in applications. A user-interface design containing any MDI windows or dialogs will automatically be generated as a full MDI application.

MDI Child Windows

The ProtoGen+ Workbench permits developers to create and register their own window classes as part of the overall application design. A window class is a set of attributes that defines how a window looks and behaves. After a class has been defined, any number of windows can be created that belong to that class.

One class is MDI child windows; another is pop-up windows (discussed next). MDI child windows contain no built-in functionality from Proto-Gen+ but instead can be edited and enhanced through custom coding. MDI child windows differ from MDI dialogs in that the MDI dialogs are automatically loaded from application resources, while MDI child windows are managed and controlled by application custom code. In effect, whatever interaction paradigm is most suitable for a given application is supported by ProtoGen+.

Pop-Up Windows

Pop-up windows are conceptually similar to MDI child windows, with one fundamental difference. MDI child windows are "clipped" to the client area of the application desktop (i.e., they operate within the overall application window), while pop-up windows aren't. Both types are supported by ProtoGen+.

Program Executables

Often it is desirable to launch an independent program from within an application. ProtoGen+ permits a menu item, button, or bitmap to do this.

Visual Coders

Visual coders include almost any type of windows object, such as common dialogs, ProtoView Screen Manager high-level functions, and C++ class objects. The ProtoGen+ Workbench comes with a standard Visual Coder, which allows Open File, Save File, Color Selection, Printer Setup, and Font dialogs to be incorporated into applications (other visual coders are available).

Function Code

The ProtoGen+ Workbench permits custom code to be entered directly within the prototyping environment. This is then included *along with* generated code to provide application custom processing. The only restriction is that the function code must be compilable in the programming language in which the application is to be generated (i.e., no Pascal function code within a C++ generation). Added function code must be compiled for it to take effect.

WORKING WITH THE PROTOGEN+ WORKBENCH

This section presents a walkthrough of how the ProtoGen+ Workbench is used to develop visual applications.

Figure 4.1 shows the ProtoGen+ Workbench. At the top is the Workbench Main Menu. Immediately underneath is a toolbar to provide the developer with quick access to commonly used ProtoGen+ Workbench functions. Underneath the toolbar is the application prototype that is being created. The application's caption, menu, and main window are presented.

At the very bottom of the Workbench is a status line, which indicates the current task being carried out, the activity status level of the ProtoView Screen Manager and SQLView (i.e., the front-end client and back-end server sides), and the current code generator that has been selected.

The first task is to open a ProtoView *application template file* (a .PVA file), which contains all of the information needed to save, reconstruct, and design the components of the Windows application. The components include the dialog resources, window class definitions, bitmaps, icons, and cursor files used within the application. The logical flow among the application's screens and the functional points (discussed earlier) to which code and objects have been attached are also part of the .PVA file configuration. In the example in Figure 4.2, the file TESTDRV.PVA contains the project information.

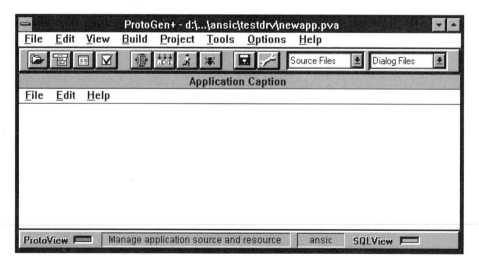

Figure 4.1 The ProtoGen+ Workbench

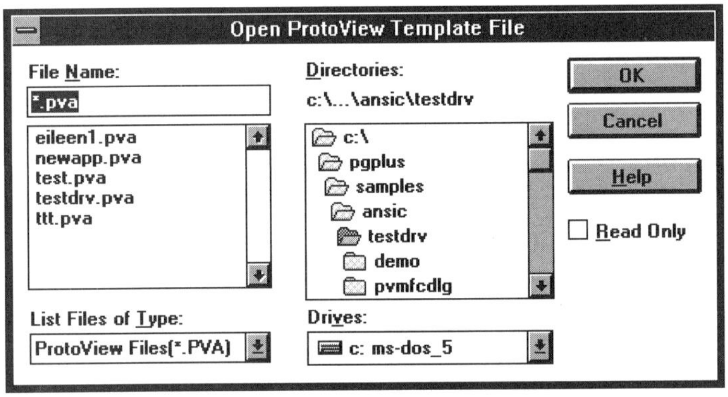

Figure 4.2 Opening an application template (.PVA) file

As with standard Microsoft Windows applications, various drives and directories may be selected (shown in Figure 4.2) to locate the desired file.

After opening the TESTDRV.PVA file, the ProtoGen+ Workbench now looks like Figure 4.3.

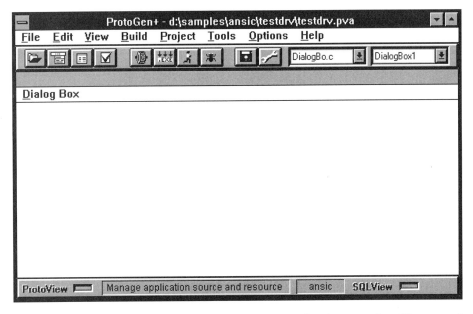

Figure 4.3 The ProtoGen+ Workbench with an application template file opened

Among the tasks that the developer would likely do to begin developing an application are:

1. Changing the application caption: Instead of the default provided by the application template file, the application caption can be modified through either a menu choice (from the EDIT menu) or by double-clicking the application caption in the Design Window. The user is presented with a simple dialog box through which the new caption can be entered.

2. Changing the main window color: Also on the EDIT menu is an option to change the color of the main window; a dialog box is presented to the user from which either basic (predefined) or custom colors may be selected (and, in the case of custom colors, defined).

3. Editing the application menu: Of more substance to the functionality of an application than the caption or the main window color is the application menu. A large portion of the initial design of a GUI client/server application is determining what commands and features should be included in the main menu. Standard Microsoft Windows guidelines (i.e., standard ordering, keyboard access through underlined unique letter mnemonics, the use of ellipses after menu items that invoke dialog boxes, etc.) should be part of the application being designed.

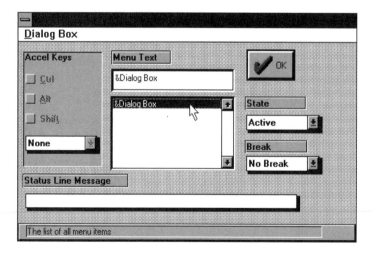

Figure 4.4 The ProtoGen+ Menu Designer

Figure 4.5 Pull-down menu for adding standard menus to an application

The ProtoGen+ Menu Designer (discussed above) is used to manage the creation of application menus. Figure 4.4 illustrates the dialog box through which this is done.

Menus from the standard application template may be deleted if they aren't needed; others may be added through a pull-down menu (Figure 4.5).

Through the dialog boxes of the Menu Designer the shell of the menus with all accelerator keys and other characteristics can be designed without any coding.

One of the powerful components of GUI applications is the ability to invoke dialog boxes from menu choices. With an already created dialog box, functionality can be added to the application (Figure 4.6).

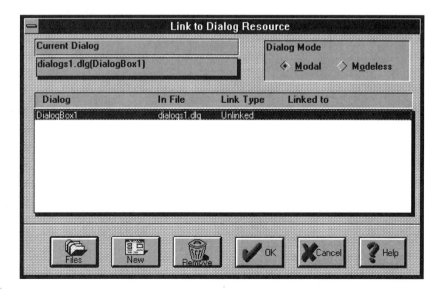

Figure 4.6 Adding dialog box functionality to an application

Figure 4.7 Accessing the standard toolbar

Another attribute of GUI applications is the use of *toolbars*. The Proto-Gen+ Workbench provides a standard Windows toolbar, which can be tailored to an individual application. Figure 4.7 illustrates how the standard toolbar is accessed prior to editing.

Toolbars may be edited (Figure 4.8) according to the needs of a given application. ViewPaint (discussed above and in more detail in Chapter 5) is used to edit any toolbar components.

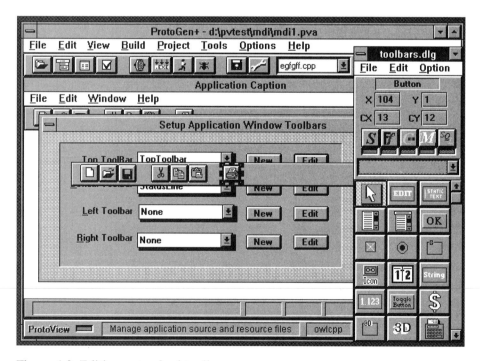

Figure 4.8 Editing a standard toolbar

TESTING (ANIMATING) AN APPLICATION

The steps briefly discussed above illustrate how simple menu and toolbar design is accomplished. One of the advantages of a visual development *environment* (as contrasted with simple screen design tools) is the ability to test-run, or "animate," the application. The ProtoGen+ Workbench permits this to be done (accomplished by clicking on one of the toolbar buttons, as detailed in the product documentation). When this happens, the Workbench toolbar and the ProtoGen+ primary menu disappear; the screen then contains only the application main window. The designer/developer can then use the mouse and keyboard to access the application menus, toolbar buttons, dialog boxes, and so forth *just as if the application were being run live (i.e., after being compiled and executed).* By doing this, any problems can be discovered early in the development process (particularly when compared with compiled 3GL code, as in traditional development environments) and changes easily made.

CODE GENERATION

Figure 4.9 illustrates some of the code generation options available from within the ProtoGen+ Workbench.

Note that as with most GUI desktop applications, code is rarely a set of self-contained, 3GL modules as in many older mainframe or minicom-

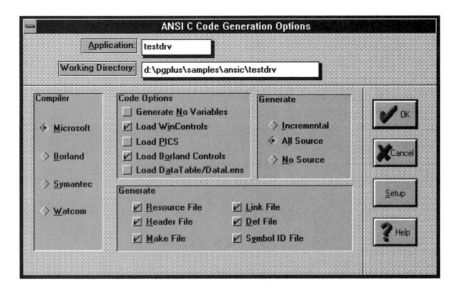

Figure 4.9 The ProtoGen+ Workbench Code Generator

puter applications, but rather many different files, each with a standard, specific purpose. The ProtoGen+ Code Generator permits the generation of resource files, header files, Symbol ID files, and the other files that are necessary for a given environment.

Applications can be compiled (an .EXE file created) directly from within the ProtoGen+ Workbench environment and can be run under the control of the Workbench also. Any debugging information that is present can also be managed through the Workbench.

FUNCTIONAL POINTS

Earlier in this chapter it was mentioned that the ProtoGen+ Workbench environment permits the linking of program controls with application functionality through the concept of functional points. This section will discuss this in more detail.

The mechanism through which functional point linkage is accomplished is as follows:

1. The specific functional point—a menu item, pushbutton, icon—is selected from the application being developed.

2. The *link to functionality* dialog is presented, from which the appropriate linkage may be chosen (Figure 4.10).

For example, as shown in Figure 4.10, functionality can be linked to a dialog box by selecting that option from the list. A screen with a list of dialog resources (Figure 4.11) is presented from which the one desired may be selected.

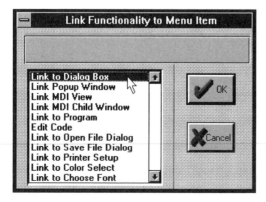

Figure 4.10 Linking functionality dialog box

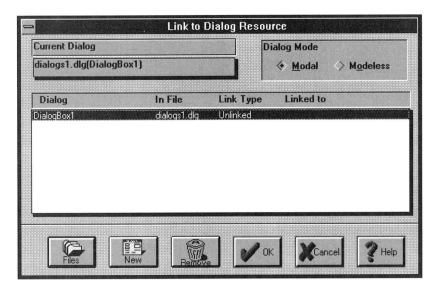

Figure 4.11 Dialog resource screen

From the list presented, each entry has a current "link status," which informs the developer as to current usage (or lack thereof) of that resource. A dialog may be already linked to some other menu, button, icon, or bitmap, or it may be linked as an MDI view. It may also be unlinked at present.

In the event that the desired dialog has not already been created, the *New* button (Figure 4.11) invokes ViewPaint, and the new dialog resource can be created and subsequently linked as required.

Alternatively, pop-up windows may be linked to a specific control; Figure 4.12 illustrates the parameters available to the user to create a pop-up window. Note that scrolling, border style, positioning, and size are among the attributes that can be specified through this dialog.

As was mentioned earlier in this chapter, similar linking can be done to MDI child windows, MDI dialogs, and program executables (examples of these are included in the ProtoGen+ documentation, referenced in Appendix B).

An example of how standard dialogs are included in and modifiable through the ProtoGen+ Workbench facilities is shown in Figure 4.13. The figure also shows how the dialog for opening files within an application can be controlled, with parameters selected at design time to control facets such as whether multiple files may or may not be selected by the application user, whether files are to be opened as read-only, whether or not "network sharing violations" are indicated to the user, and so forth.

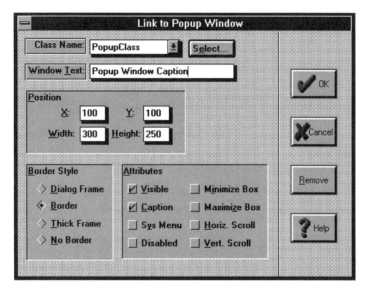

Figure 4.12 Linking to a pop-up window

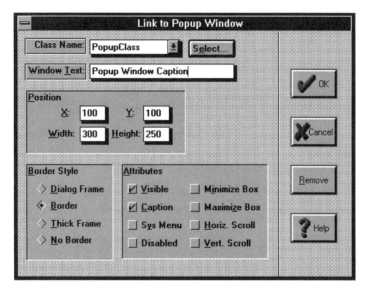

Figure 4.13 Link to OpenFile Functionality

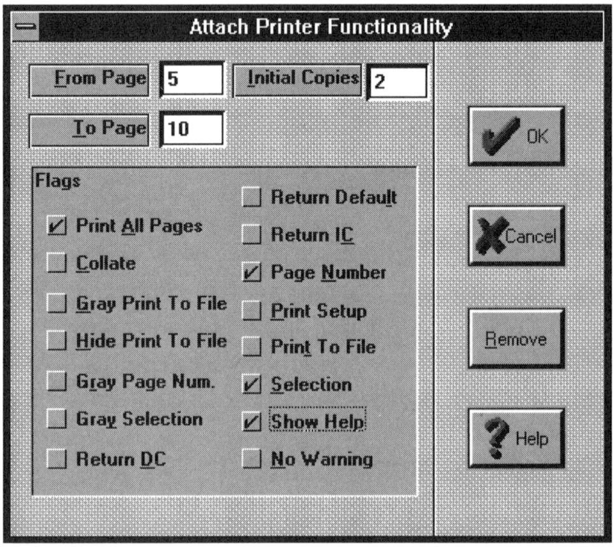

Figure 4.14 Printer functionality established for an application

The same capabilities are available to saving files, printing management (Figure 4.14), color management, and font management. These are described in detail in the product documentation.

VARIABLES AND DATA ELEMENTS

The ProtoView Screen Manager is responsible for transferring information from screens to application-resident data elements and vice versa. The styles and methods of the input fields and associated data elements are designed under ProtoGen+ to establish the necessary links to ensure interapplication component sharing of necessary variable information.

The link between data elements and screen objects involves four steps, as listed below:

1. The data element is given a name so it can be referred to in the program.
2. The data element is given a scope to determine which sections of the program can refer to that data element.
3. Data types must match.
4. Code is generated.

Each of the above items is discussed below.

Each screen object is assigned a data element name; this can take place when dialogs are being designed or from the Workbench at some subsequent time (through a menu selection). When a data element name is entered in ViewPaint and the resource is saved, the name is saved along with the dialog resource. ProtoGen+ also saves it along with the entire project. The data element saved in the dialog resource goes along wherever the dialog file goes, and it can be linked to other functional points and other applications through automatic association with the screen objects.

The data element scope—public or private—determines whether other areas of an application program can access it. Each data element's scope can be individually defined, or the default of the whole dialog (or entire application) can be used. Figure 4.15 illustrates how the scope is established.

In ViewPaint, the screen object is created with a style that determines the type of data element with which it will be interfacing. Some controls have only one type of data with which they will interface (e.g., character string only); others can interface with multiple types. Developers, for the most part, do not need to be concerned about what data types to use until the applications become increasingly sophisticated.

Finally, code generation requires that a function (vwSetFieldVar()) be called to bind a data element to a screen object. Following this step, the ProtoView Screen Manager will ensure that data are moved to and from the screen at proper times during the execution of an application (e.g., just before being initially shown to a user). The ProtoView Screen Manager will also check to ensure that screen-based editing is successful (i.e., no error condition) before moving data back from the screen objects to application variables.

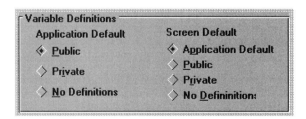

Figure 4.15 Establishing the scope of variables

MESSAGE PROCESSING

The event-driven nature of GUI software requires that applications be capable of processing numerous types of messages, including those coming back from the system with respect to the resources under management. ProtoGen+ permits application developers to choose from a wide variety of messages to be processed in the generated code that comes out of the Workbench environment. Figure 4.16 illustrates a dialog box for selecting Windows messages to be processed within the main application window.

It is important to note that the developer must write and insert the appropriate code to handle the selected messages in the manner that is desired. The absence of handling generated messages that are routed to (in the above case) the main application window could result in unpredictable run-time problems.

Very often it is desirable to add one's own messages to the standard ones handled under the operating environment. ProtoGen+ has a "custom messages" menu selection, which permits the developer to choose from messages that are custom-defined within an environment.

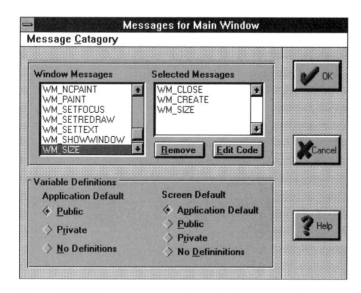

Figure 4.16 Message processing selection example

The WM_COMMAND message is the vehicle through which notification codes are sent by control objects to their parents. Events include button clicks, listbox selection or double-clicks, typing a character into an edit field, and many others. Each control type in Windows has its own set of notification codes, used to inform the dialog window procedure of events that might be of interest to the parent. For each control that is selected in the Workbench, the developer is shown the notification messages that apply to that type of control. The most common types of notification messages processed are for buttons, listboxes, and comboboxes.

Edit controls do not often need to respond to notification messages. The ProtoView Screen Manager enables keystroke editing and field-level editing to be accomplished through the VW_EDITFIELD message.

Another message that is widely used is BN_CLICKED, the primary button notification code contained within ProtoGen+. ProtoGen+ automatically generates this for applications, which means that developers never have to select a notification for a pushbutton.

MORE ABOUT THE WORKBENCH ENVIRONMENT

Figure 4.17 illustrates the toolbar of the ProtoGen+ Workbench environment.

Developing and generating applications requires that some degree of project control be established to manage the various files that comprise the application. The Manage Resource Files toolbar button invokes the

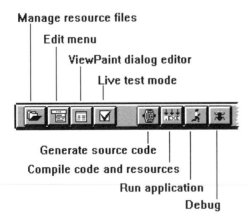

Figure 4.17 The ProtoGen+ Workbench toolbar

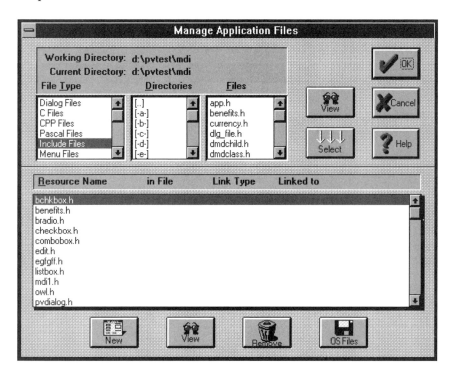

Figure 4.18 File management capabilities

dialog box shown in Figure 4.18, through which developers can control file types and various resources.

Various file types—source files, dialog files, object files, menu files, include files, library files, bitmap files, icon files, and cursor files—are managed and shown to the developer through the file type listbox. As each file type is selected, the file manager displays the resources of that type that are part of the application. As files are selected, they may be viewed by the developer through the "appropriate" editor (e.g., dialog files can be edited with ViewPaint, the standard Windows Paintbrush tool, or another designated bitmap editor can be used to view and edit bitmap files; a text editor is used for source code files; etc.). In effect, the files are treated as "peers" of one another with respect to accessibility from the Workbench.

The Select button in the dialog box causes the selected file to be added to the application. Once that occurs, it is managed and utilized in accordance with its file type. Dialog files have code generated to load and display them; include files are added to the header file of the application; bitmap files are added to the application resource file; and library files are added to the application linkage process.

The resource list shows, for dialog resources, what file contains each resource as well as the functional point to which it is linked (functional points were discussed earlier in this chapter). Before a dialog resource can be linked to a functional point, it must be selected into the application from the Manage Application Files screen shown in Figure 4.18. A dialog resource file may contain multiple dialogs, and by selecting a file all dialog resources are brought into the application and made available for linking at functional points.

Once a dialog resource has been selected into the application it then can be linked as described earlier in this chapter.

SUMMARY

This chapter has presented a consolidated overview of the ProtoGen+ Workbench development environment. In the context of developing modern client/server applications, it is essential to have a development environment in which a variety of front-end and back-end tools work in a cooperative manner. These tools, as in ProtoGen+, range from painting dialogs and screen interfaces to testing, compiling, and running applications, along with managing the back-end applications.

In the following chapters, we'll take a closer look at some of the tools and components of ProtoGen+.

5

ViewPaint

INTRODUCTION

In Chapter 4, we discussed how the ViewPaint tool of the ProtoGen+ is used to create dialogs and data entry forms. In this chapter, we'll discuss ViewPaint in more detail, giving the reader a better understanding of the mechanics behind the creation of modern client/server applications in the Windows environment.

ViewPaint is used to perform the following functions:

- edit the appearance and behavior of buttons, edit controls, bitmaps, icons, listboxes, scroll bars, and toolbars
- incorporate custom controls into Windows client/server applications
- customize the colors and fonts used for individual dialog components
- designate background bitmaps for data entry forms and make them scrollable both vertically and horizontally
- establish a dynamic status line for dialog windows using point and click design
- specify help message text strings or help topics for individual controls and buttons

- establish editing criteria and data validation requirements for dialog window objects

In the previous chapter we discussed the use of the ProtoGen+ Workbench and the invocation of various editors and tools from that environment. ViewPaint can be invoked in that manner or, alternatively, run as a stand-alone application.

Before further discussion about ViewPaint functionality, it is important to clarify the definition of *resources* in a Windows context. Resources are data objects that are kept separate from the main body of code in a Windows application, permitting modification and management more easily than if hard-coded into the application's code. Typically, resources appear in two forms. One is as a text file, containing descriptions of the resource object. The other is the binary equivalent form of the verbal description; this latter form is achieved after compilation by a special resource compiler that is "Windows-literate," that is, it understands the form and format of each type of Windows resource.

THE VIEWPAINT ENVIRONMENT

Figure 5.1 shows the ViewPaint environment. The major areas include:

- the Design Window
- the Alignment Palette
- the Control Panel
- the Tools Palette

Each is discussed below.

The Design Window

The large, empty white space in Figure 5.1 is known as the Design Window and is where dialogs and data entry screens are painted. The design window may be resized either larger or smaller, depending on the needs of a given application. The standard Windows resizing mechanisms (i.e., "grabbing" a "drag area" on the perimeter of a window) are used to control the size.

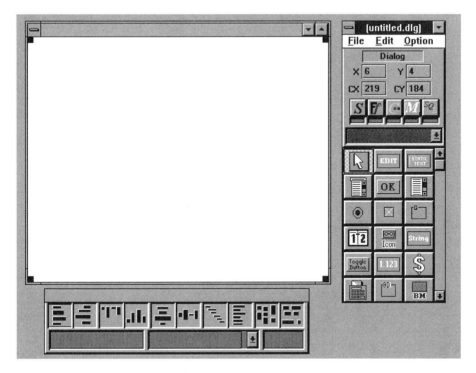

Figure 5.1 The ViewPaint environment

The Alignment Palette

One of the frustrating things about visually designing client application screens is that due to the visual nature, alignment of the various controls can often be imprecise as compared to the code-based entry of coordinates. The Alignment Palette gives the designer of the client application ten different predetermined alignment formats that may be chosen to guide the alignment of those controls.

The predefined alignment options include:

- Align vertically left—the selected set of controls within the Design Window will be aligned evenly on their respective left sides.

- Align vertically right—the same as above, except aligned evenly on their respective right sides.

- Align horizontally top—the selected items are aligned evenly along their respective top borders.

- Align horizontally bottom—the selected items are aligned evenly with the bottom borders in synchronization with one another.
- Center horizontally—the controls' respective centers are aligned, top to bottom.
- Center vertically—the controls' respective centers are aligned from left to right.
- Spread even horizontally—the selected controls are evenly spaced in the horizontal plane.
- Spread even vertically—the selected controls are evenly spaced in the vertical plane.
- Make equal field width—the widths of the selected controls are adjusted so that all are equal, and all controls in the group are adjusted to equal the width of the anchor field control in the selected group.
- Make equal field height—the same as above, except all the heights are adjusted equal to one another.

The Control Panel

The Control Panel is the primary window into which commands are entered and through which the visual design process is managed. Figure 5.2 shows the Control Panel and the various components. Note that the SQLView tool (discussed in Chapter 7) used to manage the data side of the client/server application is accessible from the Control Panel.

Figure 5.2 The ViewPaint Control Panel

Figure 5.3 The ViewPaint Tools Palette

The Tools Palette

Figure 5.3 illustrates the Tools Palette and the various controls. Some of these will be described in this chapter with respect to their functionality; the reader is directed to the ProtoGen+ and ViewPaint documentation for more details.

The next section contains some details about how the various controls in the Tools Palette are used to develop client/server applications.

THE TOOLS PALETTE CONTROLS

The following subsections contain descriptions of the various Tools Palette icons. Refer to Figure 5.3 for illustrations of each.

Edit Text

Application portions that require users to enter text input are managed through the Edit Text icon. The styles of the Edit control are changed through the Edit Class Styles dialog, as shown in Figure 5.4.

Through the use of this dialog, the developer sets the characteristics of fields into which data are entered (again, as with the other facilities, without having to code). Among the class styles are:

- multiline input and display (as contrasted with single-line input and display)

- vertical and/or horizontal scrolling controls

- automatic vertical and horizontal scrolling on input (i.e., if the text being entered exceeds the size of the field)

- upper- or lowercase—to force all text entered into the desired case, irrespective of how the application user enters it

- password control—instead of echoing the text characters entered, asterisks are used to protect sensitive information such as passwords

- read only—for display-only (i.e., no user input permitted) text controls

- grouping of controls (for navigation by use of the arrow keys)

- a variety of 3D styles

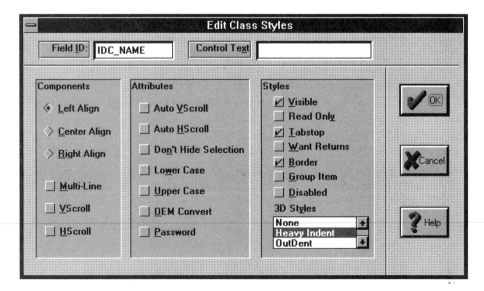

Figure 5.4 Edit Class Styles dialog

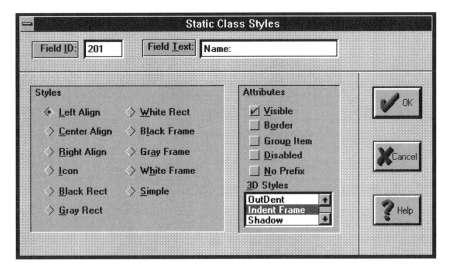

Figure 5.5 Static Class Styles

Static Text

Static text is text that is displayed on a window but cannot be edited by the user. Static constructs can also be used to display an icon, a shaded rectangle, or a simple frame in which to group items.

The Static Text class has a variety of looks and attributes, including three-dimensional looks for indented, outdented, frame indent, or shadow styles. Figure 5.5 illustrates the Static Class Styles dialog.

Note that text can be positioned (aligned) within a field according to the designer's preference (left, right, or center). An icon (identified by a name that relates to a definition elsewhere in the resource file) can be specified. A variety of aesthetic styles (different frames or rectangles) can also be specified.

Button Classes

Like most GUI applications, those designed by using ViewPaint can have a variety of different buttons, which can be used according to the needs of an individual control. Check boxes (for multiple selections), radio buttons (typically for a single selection), and pushbuttons (to invoke something) are among the button classes. Figure 5.6 illustrates the Button Class Styles dialog.

Note that a "3 State Button" can be specified. This button looks the same as a check box, but the control can also be grayed (dimmed, indicat-

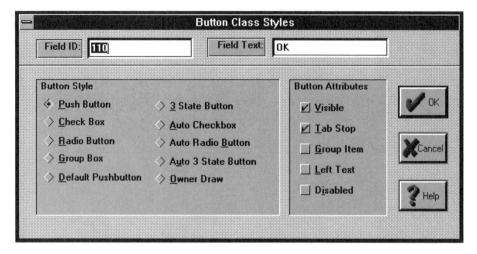

Figure 5.6 Button Class Styles

ing that the state of the check box is not determined) for some selection range (i.e., some selections may be "on" while others are "off").

Auto check boxes and auto radio buttons are single-instance controls (i.e., only one choice is presented),which are either set (filled) or unset (open).

Note also that ViewPaint permits the creation of "owner-drawn buttons," controlled by sending a **WM_MEASUREITEM** message to the owner window when a visual aspect of the button changes.

Navigation among buttons is specified by the various attributes in the dialog, including how the TAB and arrow keys function.

Listbox Controls

Listboxes present application users with a list of items from which one or more selections (according to what is specified by the designer/developer) can be made. Figure 5.7 illustrates the Listbox Class Dialog.

As with the other control dialogs examined previously in this chapter, the designer or developer can simply check off the attributes and styles of the listbox he or she wants to create. A standard listbox (specified by the first control in the Styles group) automatically sorts strings in the listbox (when "Sort" is selected), and operates in a standard click/double-click paradigm common to GUI applications.

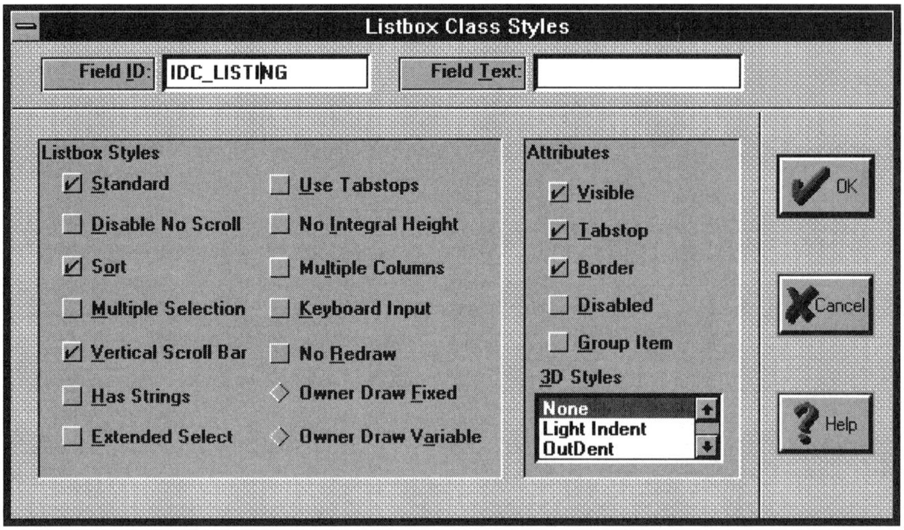

Figure 5.7 Listbox Class Dialog

The presence of a vertical scroll bar is also specified by the control, and two different scrolling (or, more specifically, "no scrolling") visual paradigms can be specified. By checking the "Disable No Scroll" control the vertical scroll bar is shown as disabled (grayed) when not enough items are in the list to scroll. Leaving that control unselected hides the vertical scroll. The designer can choose whatever visual paradigm is standard in his or her organization's applications, or tailor the view to a specific application as necessary.

Many times, application users need to be able to select multiple entries from the list at one time. The "Multiple Selection" control automatically enables or disables this capability according to the functionality of any given application listbox. The "Extended Select" control permits the keyboard's shift key to be used for multiple selection ranges.

When necessary, a multiple-column listbox can also be specified; the width of the columns can be specified by an LB_SETCOLUMNWIDTH message.

Comboboxes

A Combobox is a means by which edit strings and drop-down controls can be managed together (i.e., presenting the user with a list of selections

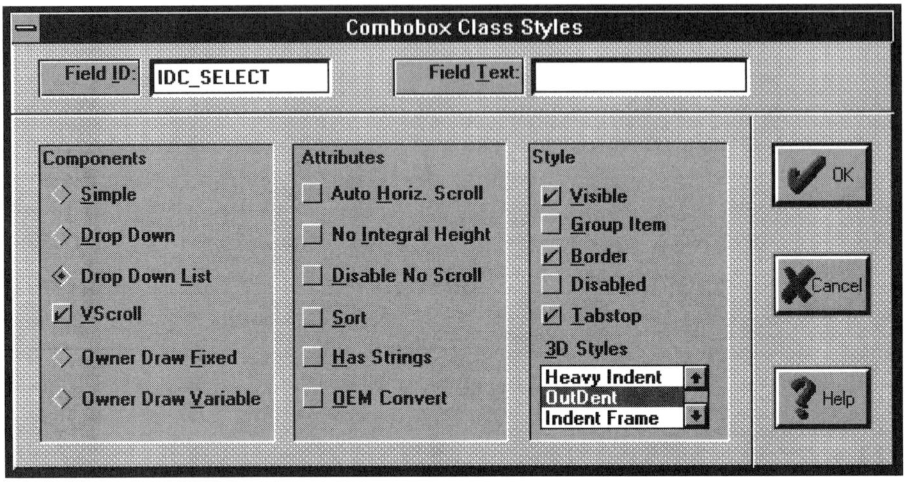

Figure 5.8 The Combobox Class Style dialog

for entry into an edit field). Figure 5.8 illustrates the Combobox Class dialog.

Toggle Buttons (pvButton Styles)

A toggle button is a pushbutton control that is either pushed (i.e., "set") or not pushed ("off"). The dialog for this control (Figure 5.9) shows the settings that can be selected by the developer (button size and various styles).

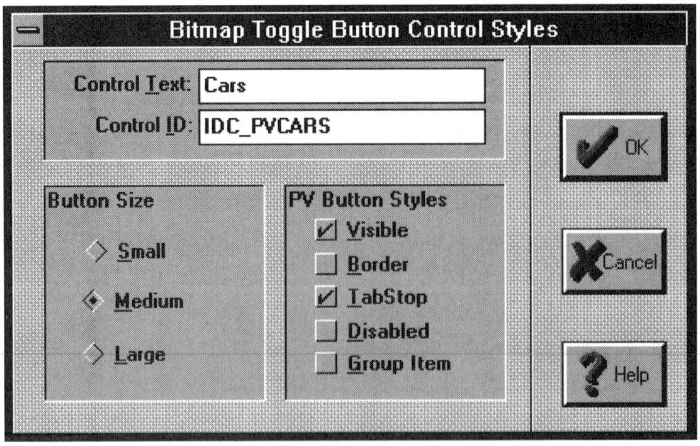

Figure 5.9 Bitmap Toggle Button (pvButton) Control Styles dialog

**Figure 5.10 The color management
control within an application**

Color Selection

Color selection controls may be presented to the users of applications for adjusting window colors, changing the default colors of various objects, changing colors of items during the execution of the application, and so on. The control is a set of three slider bars (Figure 5.10) with Red, Green, and Blue (RGB) color values.

The Color Control Class dialog (not shown here) is a relatively simple one, with only a few controls (e.g., whether or not a border is present around the color control, the degree of indentation of the control, etc.).

String Controls

ViewPaint permits developers to use a ProtoView custom edit control (pvString Style), which can be set to accept only alphabetic, only numeric, or alphanumeric input. Case conversions (all upper, all lower) can also be set. Figure 5.11 shows the String Control Styles dialog.

Dates

Another custom control—pvDate—permits the display and editing of dates to be automatically specified by the developer without the need for any programming. The format (i.e., MMDDYY, MMDDYYYY, DDMMYY, etc.) desired for a given application window can be specified, the type of separator (slashes, dashes, dots) can likewise be noted, and border and group item control options can be selected. Figure 5.12 illustrates the Date Control Styles dialog.

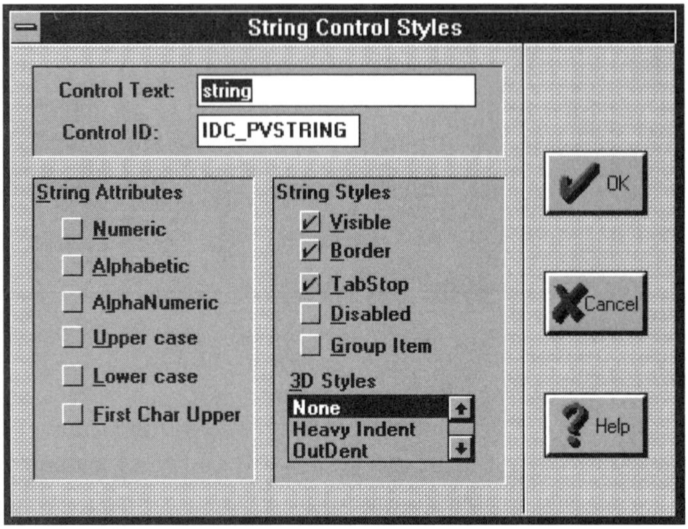

Figure 5.11 The String Control Styles dialog

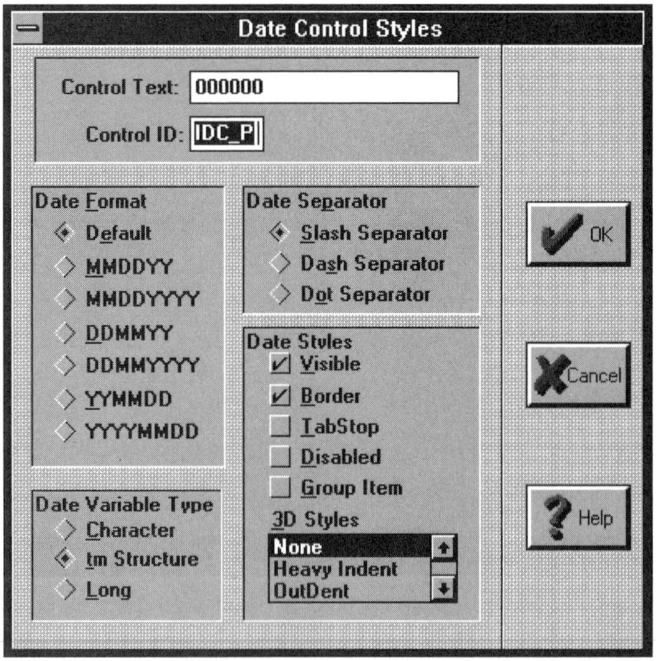

Figure 5.12 The Date Control Styles dialog

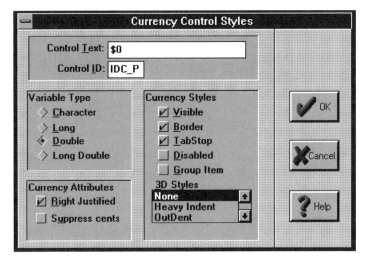

Figure 5.13 The Currency Control Styles dialog

Currency, Numeric, and Real Styles

Other custom controls are available for currency data (e.g., the variable type that will be used, whether or not cents are shown, and if the variable should be right-justified or not), and for numeric and real data. The control class dialogs for each of these three custom controls are similar to one another (Figure 5.13 illustrates the one for currency control).

Bitmaps and Icons

Often it is desirable to use visual items in an application—either a bitmap picture or an on-screen icon—to launch dialogs or even other applications (as was discussed in Chapter 4). Custom controls are available to permit bitmaps (.BMP files) and icons (.ICO files) to be included within the realm of a client/server application. The control dialogs permit the developer to specify positioning of the bitmaps or icons relative to control text (the text to be to the top, bottom, left, or right, respectively, of the graphical image), whether a single mouse click (instead of a double-click) can be used to invoke that control, and similar items).

Ticker Controls

The ticker control operates as a "stock ticker" does, moving text within its client area from right to left. By using this control, the developer using ViewPaint can design application windows that have either static messages or dynamically updated data "floating" in front of the application's users.

CONTROL METHODS

During the execution of the application, the on-screen controls devised by the designers and developers (such as those described in the previous section) are used to gather information from the user. The ProtoView Screen Manager (discussed in Chapter 6) provides substantial assistance in the overall program development process in addition to ViewPaint, interacting with the controls on a view window to update application variables when buttons are clicked, for example.

VeiwPaint provides a set of *control method dialogs*, which are used by the developer to select the properties, actions, validations, and formats that are applied to the various controls. This section gives a brief overview of the various dialogs the application developer can use.

Invoking the Select Methods Capability

While painting a screen of controls, the application developer using View-Paint would set methods in the following manner:

1. Choose the control for which a method is to be defined.
2. Either double-click or press the right mouse button.
3. Choose Select Methods from the floating menu that he or she is given.

Figure 5.14 illustrates the above process.

Depending on the type of control for which the methods are being defined (i.e., edit controls, static text controls, etc., as discussed in the previous section), the developer is presented with a tailored dialog box in which various attributes and capabilities can be specified. These are illustrated and briefly discussed in the following subsections. Again, the most important item to note with respect to the functionality is the visual, nonprogramming nature of the application development process. Help messages, error messages, interfaces with other services, and many other

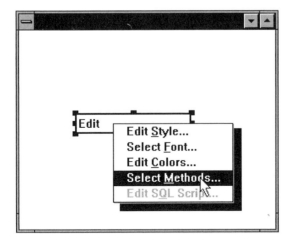

Figure 5.14 Selecting methods for a control

facets of the controls can be specified in a manner just as visually oriented as the point and click screen painting capabilities discussed earlier in this chapter.

String Control Methods

Figure 5.15 illustrates the pvString Fields Methods dialog box.

Among the characteristics that can be defined for the string management method are:

- Mandatory or optional fields—can the user leave the field without entering any data. This is a valuable on-the-spot validation capability, which "forces" the entry of complete data as needed within a form or other control.

- Protected (display-only, no update) text.

- Excluding certain characters from input—by using the "Exclude Characters" edit control in the dialog box (which invokes the @EX-CLUDE method), the user is prohibited from entering any characters specified by the developer. Using the "Include Characters" (@INCLUDE method) edit control prohibits the entry of any characters *except* those specified by the developer. The application user will hear a beep if excluded characters are entered.

- Edit masks—by using the *, #, @, and ? characters an edit mask of permissible alphanumeric entries can be created (i.e., any character,

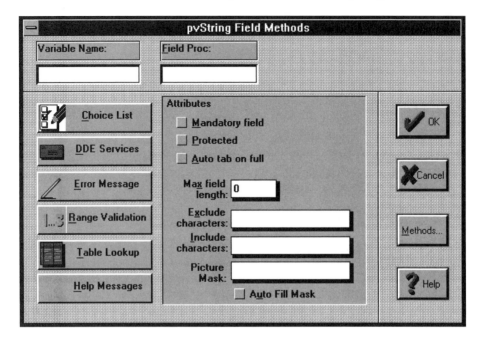

Figure 5.15 The pvString Field Methods dialog box

only digits, only alphabetic, or only alphanumeric and spaces, respectively).

- Choice lists—commonly known as "list of values," the choice list is a set of permissible entries into a field. For example, if entry is being made for the type of medal won by an athlete in an international competition, the developer could specify that permissible entries are GOLD, SILVER, and BRONZE.

- DDE services—fields can be set up to communicate using Microsoft Windows Dynamic Data Exchange (DDE) capabilities. The DDE links can be established with other Windows programs (e.g., Microsoft Excel) or with other applications created by the ProtoView environment. Within the ViewPaint test mode and ProtoGen+, the DDE links are live, meaning that applications can be checked out with respect to the DDE links. Whether the specified item is a DDE client or server is specified directly within the dialog (Figure 5.16).

- Error messages—three different types of error messages can be specified for a string control: balloon messages (a rounded rectangle appearing beneath the control—this is the default), a message box,

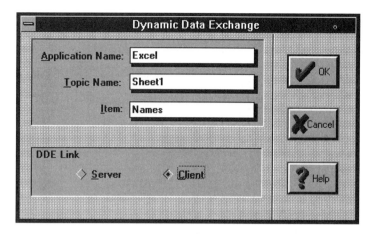

Figure 5.16 The Dynamic Data Exchange dialog

or a status line message. The text of the error messages is also entered by the developer.

- Help messages—context-sensitive help can be linked to individual fields and buttons.

- Range validation—in addition to "standard" range validation (e.g., all positive numbers, a number between 10 and 100, etc.), ViewPaint permits multiple lower and upper range bounds to be specified for a single control (e.g., 10–20, 30–40, 5,000–10,000, 20,000–25,000, 80,000–100,000, etc.). This is often useful for data entry for numeric "code items" (i.e., ranges of different permissible message IDs).

- Table lookup—dynamic validation against table-based data can be specified for strings. File names and coordinates within the table are specified by the developer while designing the application.

Editbox Control Methods

The dialog box for the editbox control method specification is identical to that of the string control (previous subsection).

Listbox Control Methods

The dialog for listbox control is shown in Figure 5.17.

A couple of items are worth noting. The "Initial Item Selection" control, when checked, selects the item in the listbox based on the offset in an

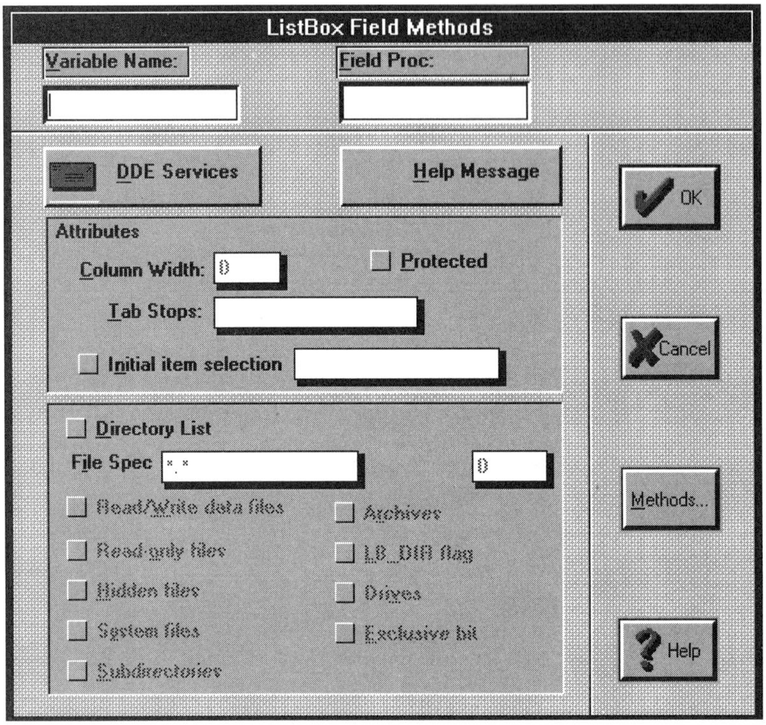

Figure 5.17 The ListBox Field Methods dialog

LBARRAY structure at run time or, alternatively, a value based on the string or numeric value entered into the edit control in the dialog shown in Figure 5.17.

The "Directory List" check box makes available all of the choices in the group box. To fill the listbox from a directory listing (e.g., the names of a group of files), the developer enters a DOS wild-card command (e.g., *.c for "C" language source files). The other check boxes in that portion of the dialog are used for other measures of file control (e.g., displaying drives, subdirectories, read-only files, system and hidden files, etc.).

Pushbutton Control Methods

Figure 5.18 illustrates the Pushbutton Control dialog.

Note that the controls are used to specify:

- the file name where a graphical image (bitmap or icon) can be found
- text for the button

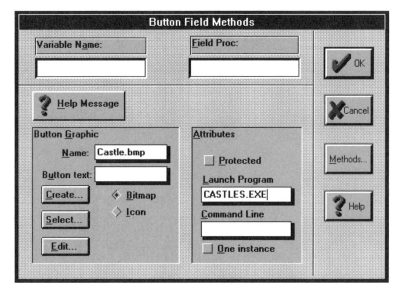

Figure 5.18 The Button Field Methods dialog

- the file name of an executable program to be launched
- design-time creation of the graphical image (by the Create pushbutton)
- help message controls and text for that control

Currency Control Methods

The edit control methods form the basis for the currency control methods (e.g., the choice list, or list of acceptable values, is used to specify permissible entries), with the additional factor of being able to select a country with which currency values will be associated. The default is U.S. dollars, but French francs, Mexican pesos, and other currencies can be selected.

Icon Control Methods

Associated help messages, the invocation of an executable program to be launched, and command lines (e.g., passing file names or other parameters to an invoked program) can be specified through the icon control method dialog.

Other Control Methods

The other controls discussed in the previous section (dates, numerics and reals, tables, etc.) all have a set of associated methods that are "programmed" in the same manner as those described above (i.e., selecting a control on the design palette and bringing up the dialog for that control). Most of the remaining dialogs are similar to those discussed above (specifically, edit and string, with the specification of ranges of values, choice lists, associated help and error messages, etc.). The reader is directed to the ViewPaint documentation for complete details regarding the functionality of each of these controls.

SUMMARY

This chapter has presented an overview of the ProtoGen+ ViewPaint Dialog Editor, a visual development environment through which dialogs can be designed and developed and through which a great deal of functionality can be incorporated into the flow of the application . . . all without the need for traditional programming. As has been mentioned previously, the interested reader is directed to the ProtoGen+ ViewPaint documentation for further information.

The next chapter will discuss another facility of the ProtoGen+ environment—the ProtoView Screen Manager.

6

The ProtoView Screen Manager

INTRODUCTION

ProtoView Screen Manager is a functional layer between Windows and the application being developed. This chapter will discuss this component of the ProtoGen+ environment.

COMPONENTS

ProtoView Screen Manager is made up of several distinct components, which interact with one another. These are:

- the ProtoView Dynamic Link Library (DLL)
- the WinControl control library

The ProtoView Screen Manager offloads a great deal of the repetitive and time-consuming programming effort, enabling the application developer to concentrate on the business/application logic of the program being developed. WinControl (discussed in Chapter 8) classes work with the ProtoView Screen Manager.

VIEWS

A view is a program object that controls the look and feel of a window containing a set of child window field controls. A view is an object in that it maintains a private data structure for the view and a set of both public and private functions that can act upon the view data structure.

A view can be thought of as an interface between an application program and Windows; it is a repository of window information maintained on behalf of the application program. The view structure contains information relating to the characteristics of the view as a whole, as well as a list of field controls belonging to the view and their characteristics and properties. The information stored in the view structure can be accessed or changed by an application program throughout the life span of the view.

At some point after it is created, the view window must be displayed. This usually occurs after variables have been linked to data entry fields, field subclassing functions have been attached to fields needing special control over editing or appearance, field methods have been established, and field styles have been set.

After the view is shown on the screen, the user is then in control, putting the view window to work to carry out the purpose for which it was created.

The life of the view comes to an end when the view is destroyed. Destroying the view is accomplished differently depending on whether the view is modal, modeless, or an MDI view. At that point all memory allocated for the view and field controls is returned to the system.

All view access must be accomplished through the API provided, because the ProtoView Screen Manager is implemented as a DLL. The set of functions in ProtoView Screen Manager (currently 175) is available to developers for managing views.

The fields (e.g., the pushbuttons, edit fields, etc., which were discussed in the previous chapter with respect to ViewPaint) respond to messages from the view and notify the Screen Manager of events of interest. ProtoView Screen Manager controls movement between fields and views, always checking with the current field control before moving focus to a new control.

In general, ProtoView Screen Manager views are just like ordinary Microsoft Windows windows except that the facilities provided within the Screen Manager can be used instead of having to do all window management entirely by the application program logic.

CONTROLS

ProtoView controls interact with the application programs, as discussed earlier. The ProtoView Screen Manager is responsible for updating the controls in the dialog from application variables before displaying the field windows.

The primary way in which an application program interfaces with a field control in the Screen Manager is through a data element or variable. For example, the edit class interfaces with a data structure of type (char *), and the address of the character string is specified in either the vwSetField() or vwSetFieldVar() function call. Thereafter, ProtoView Screen Manager automatically ensures that the data structure is updated periodically as the user enters data on the screen.

The documentation for the ProtoView Screen Manager contains code examples for associating variables with controls.

PROGRAMMING

In the development flow, programming with the ProtoView Screen Manager usually occurs after the application windows have been painted (using ViewPaint, as discussed in the previous chapter) and generated from the ProtoGen+ Workbench. At this point, the user interface is nearly complete. Colors, subclassing functions, field methods, and bitmap graphics can be incorporated without having to access the ProtoView Screen Manager function libraries directly. Additionally, SQLView (Chapter 7) can be used to implement and test database queries as the screen flows are being designed.

Data entry fields in ProtoView Screen Manager are implemented as Windows controls. The six standard Windows controls (edit, button, static, listbox, combobox, and scroll bar) are available in ProtoView Screen Manager programs, along with other specialized ones (e.g., pvString, pvNumeric, pvDate, pvIcon, pvBitmap, pvCurrency, pvTable, pvReal, pvColor).

The code segments for the ProtoView Screen Manager field controls reside in a DLL called WINCTL.DLL. Each control has two functions associated with it, one being a function that is called once when the DLL is initially loaded (to register the control class), and the other being the default field proc, whose job it is to handle messages sent by Windows to the field control. The way in which the default field proc responds to the various messages it receives determines the nature, style, and capabilities of the field.

Through function subclassing, ProtoView Screen Manager provides a convenient way for applications to intercept messages bound for the default field proc and to process them in different ways. An application can designate its own function to receive Windows messages (by a parameter in either the vwSetField or vwSetFieldProc function); the designated function can then filter the messages bound for the field control, processing those of interest and disregarding the others.

ProtoView Screen Manager provides automatic application variable updates for fields that have been associated with an application variable of the proper type. The contents of the application variable are converted to window text for display just before a view is first shown. Then, when the view is ready to be destroyed, the application variable is updated from the window text. The conversion from screen to application takes place automatically only if an OK button has been established for the view; otherwise, the application must direct variable updating through the use of vwUpdateApp().

In between these two conversions, an application can do any number of conversions from application to screen and back using the functions vwUpdateScreen() and vwUpdateApp(). The data typing must match between controls and variables (e.g., integer data types for buttons, character arrays for string controls, etc.). The ProtoGen+ code generators will generate the proper data types for variables added through its interfaces but when creating variables dynamically, it is important to know exactly what type of variable must be created for a given class and style of field control.

More about Subclassing

As was mentioned earlier, function subclassing is an integral part of not only ProtoView Screen Manager but Windows. Very often, it is a difficult concept for traditional mainframe 3GL (e.g., COBOL, FORTRAN) programmers to grasp, but when developing open client/server applications it is something that needs to be learned.

Through subclassing, it is possible to modify the behavior of a Proto-View Screen Manager class object. The subclassing function intercepts messages intended for the function that is responsible for the behavior of the subclassed object and can decide how to respond to the message.

In general, there are three actions the subclassing function can take. These are:

1. The message can be passed on to the subclassed function without taking any action whatsoever. A Windows control contains a default window function, which handles most of the messages processed by the field. Messages not processed by the control's own window procedure are passed on to DefWindowProc(). If the developer decides to subclass the default message processing function by specifying a field proc, it must be decided which messages need to be processed and which messages the default window procedure should process.

2. The subclassing function can trap the message and handle it appropriately and then pass the message on to the subclassed function.

3. The subclassing function can trap the message, take appropriate action, and then return, without passing the message to the subclassed function at all.

Superclassing

When superclassing is used, an entirely new Windows class is created for an object, but the new class borrows from a class that already exists, such as the edit control or the listbox class. This is accomplished by calling the window procedure of the old class for most of the basic behavior of the control. The superclass then just adds logic and processing where the old class lacks the required support. In general, superclassing can be thought of as conceptually similar to C++ inheritance.

Callback Functions

Sometimes, it is desirable for a module in a DLL to call a function within an application. Reasons include having to provide additional information to the library function or having to provide specialized services within the application that are not supported by the library routine. ProtoView Screen Manager has examples of both of these situations. A callback function is used when an application wishes to customize high-level functions such as vwEditFile() or vwBrowse(). In these instances, the function address of the callback is passed in with the function call and is then used by the ProtoView Screen Manager to pass Windows messages so that custom processing can take place.

All Windows procedures, view procedures, and field procedures are considered to be callback functions. These functions are called from outside the application, either by Windows or by ProtoView Screen Manager.

Dialog Coordinates

Another task of ProtoView Screen Manager is to handle the coordinates on a screen of dialogs, allowing for different types of monitors to be used. Dialog coordinates are derived from the characteristics of the system font, which is managed by Windows through the video device driver to ensure that screens are legible on a given monitor type.

Dialog coordinates can be converted to screen coordinates and back using the ProtoView Screen Manager functions vwDialogToScreen() and vwScreenToDialog(). Both of these functions take a pointer to a RECT structure as a parameter.

BUILDING PROTOVIEW SCREEN MANAGER APPLICATIONS

Client/server GUI applications can make calls to both Windows and ProtoView Screen Manager to accomplish the tasks that need to be done. There are some distinctions (e.g., ProtoView Screen Manager functions require a handle to a view as a parameter, while Windows functions require a handle to a window), but in general the calling conventions are similar to one another.

All ProtoView Screen Manager functions are prefixed with the letters "vw," followed by a verb, the object to be acted upon, and ending with the attribute to be acted upon. Examples have been used in this chapter, and others are:

- vwSetViewCaption()
- vwSetOKButton()

This section will include code examples to give the reader some idea of the construction of ProtoView Screen Manager applications.

Example #1

In this example, ViewPaint (Chapter 5) is used to paint controls and the ViewPaint code generator is used. The application components are as follows:

Header File

```
// Example1 .h Header File
#define              FILENAME 16
char Filename[FILENAME + 1];
```

WinMain() Function

```
// Example1 Source File
// Example1 .c  ProtoView Screen Manager Tutorial example
#include" pv.h"
#include" Example1 .h"
//View handle and window handle declarations
VIEW Example1;
HWND  hWndExample1;
int   WINAPI WinMain(HINSTANCE hInstance,
                          HINSTANCE hPrevInstance,
                          LPSTR lpszCmdLine,
                          WORD nCmdShow)
{
static char szAppName[] = Example1";
MSG msg;
    Example1  = wvCreateView(hInstance,
                                "Example1",
                                NULL,
                                NULL,
                                NULL);
    wvSetFieldVar(Example1, 1, Filename);
    hWndExample1 = wvShowView(Example1);
    while(GetMessage(&msg,NULL,0,0))
        TranslateMessage(&msg);
        DispatchMessage(&msg);
    return msg.wParam;
}
```

Resource File

```
//Example1.rc Resource File
#include style.h
#include wwstyle.h
rcinclude EXAMPLE1.dlg  // template file containing the screen resource.
```

Dialog Resource File

```
Example1.dlg  ProtoView Screen Manager Template File
Example1 DIALOG LOADONCALL MOVEABLE DISCARDABLE 67, 54, 175, 68
STYLE WS_POPUP | WS_VISIBLE | WS_DLGFRAME
BEGIN
    CONTROL "&Enter Filename:", 104, "static", WS_CHILD, 25, 16, 0, 0 END
    CONTROL , 101, pvString, WS_CHILD, 87, 16, 65, 8  /*Filename,*/
    CONTROL "OK", 102, Button, WS_CHILD | BS_OKAY, 24, 32, 49, 16
    CONTROL  "Cancel", 103, Button, WS_CHILD | BS_CANCEL, 88, 32, 49, 16
END
```

Module Definition File

```
NAME  Example1
DESCRIPTION 'ProtoView Screen Manager Tutorial example'
STUB 'WINSTUB.EXE'
CODE MOVEABLE DATA MOVEABLE MULTIPLE PRELOAD
EXETYPE Windows
HEAPSIZE 1024
STACKSIZE 8192
EXPORTS
    Example1WndProc
```

Some items worth noting with respect to the example above are:

1. The program calls vwCreateView(), passing it the name "Example1" of the view dialog resource (in the Dialog Resource File). This function will then locate the dialog resource that is needed, read it in, and process each statement to create the window that had been designed in ViewPaint.

2. The vwSetFieldVar() function is called in the WinMain() function to associate a variable with the file name field control. This allows ProtoView Screen Manager to update this variable after the user finishes entering data into the view.

3. The vwShowView() function is called (also within WinMain()) to display the example to the user; this function is passed the handle of the view to be shown.

4. Once the view window is created and shown, the program goes into a message retrieval loop and dispatches the messages to the Example1 window procedure, which processes them. If the user either clicks on the OK or CANCEL button (or presses the RETURN or ESCAPE key), the Example1 dialog box will be automatically destroyed. If the user presses RETURN or clicks OK, the data the user had typed in for a file name will be retained in the string variable called Filename. Pressing ESCAPE or clicking CANCEL means that no data will be saved.

Example #2

Note that ProtoGen+ supports a "mix and match" development paradigm, that is, it isn't necessary that ViewPaint be used.

WinMain() Function

Note that in this example a number of ProtoView Screen Manager function calls are used in the source code that hadn't been used in the previous example.

```
    /* EXAMPLE2.c -- ProtoView Screen Manager Tutorial example */

    #include <windows.h>
    #include <time.h>
    #include "pvplus.h"
    #include "Example2.h"

    /* Handles to View and View Window */
    VIEW    Example2;
    HWND    hWndExample2;

int WINAPI WinMain(HINSTANCE hInstance,
                   HINSTANCEh PrevInstance,
                   LPSTR lpszCmdLine,
                   int nCmdShow)
{
  static char szAppName[] = "Example2";
  MSG    msg;

  Example2 = wvOpenView(hInstance, NULL, WS_POPUP | WS_VISIBLE | WS_DLGFRAME,
                        NULL,
                        NULL,
                        NULL);

  vvSetField(Example2, -1, "static", "", WS_CHILD | WS_VISIBLE | SS_LEFT, 87, 16, 65, 12,
                        Filename,
                        NULL);
  vvSetField(Example2, ID_FILENAME, "pvString", "",
                        WS_CHILD | WS_VISIBLE | WS_BORDER,
                        87, 16, 65, 12,
                        Filename,
                        NULL);
  vvSetField(Example2, IDOK, "button", "OK",
                        WS_CHILD | WS_VISIBLE | BS_DEFPUSHBUTTON,
                        64, 48, 46, 16, NULL, NULL);

  vvSetOKButton(Example2, IDOK);

  vvSetField(Example2, IDCANCEL, "button", "Cancel",
                        WS_CHILD | WS_VISIBLE | BS_PUSHBUTTON,
                        141, 49, 46, 16, NULL, NULL);

vvSetCancelButton(Example2, IDCANCEL);

  vvSetFieldString(Example2,1,"@ALPHANUM,@MND,@MSG(Enter filename);");
  vvSetViewPosition(Example2, 67, 52, 242, 121, VW_DLGCOORD);

  hWndExample2 = wvShowView(Example2);

  while(GetMessage(&msg, NULL, 0, 0))
  {
        TranslateMessage(&msg);
        DispatchMessage(&msg);
  }
  return msg.wParam;
}.
```

SUMMARY

This chapter has provided a brief overview of the ProtoView Screen Manager component of ProtoGen+. The *ProtoView Screen Manager User's Guide and Reference* contains significantly more details, including a programmer's reference for the various function calls available to application developers. The primary purpose of our discussion is to get a general idea of how ProtoView Screen Manager fits into the desktop client application development area.

In the next chapter, we'll shift our attention away from the client application side of the ProtoGen+ environment to the database server side as we discuss SQLView.

7

SQLView Visual Database Access

INTRODUCTION

In this chapter our ProtoGen+ discussion shifts from the client side to SQLView, a development tool for the database server side of a multitiered client/server application. SQLView is a dynamic link library (DLL), which allows database developers to link ProtoView controls (discussed in the previous chapters) to assigned database columns and actions. The interface is accomplished through the use of middleware, such as Q+E Software's QELib and Microsoft's Open Database Connectivity (ODBC) APIs. Through the use of field and view methods, SQLView will pull data values from ProtoView controls, build and issue SQL statements, and retrieve data from linked columns back to the controls.

Simple database applications can be developed using the ProtoGen+ development environment (e.g., ViewPaint and the editors and generators) and SQLView. More complex applications can use the SQLView API to handle connection management, error processing, and free-form SQL issuance.

The database-connected dialogs are created in ViewPaint just as general dialogs are. ViewPaint links field controls to database columns, and action buttons are linked to SQL action scripts. At run time, SQLView is capable of building and issuing SQL INSERT, DELETE, UPDATE, and SELECT

SQL statements based on the data contained in the view's controls, as well as resolving parameters within and issuing custom SQL scripts.

SQLVIEW STRUCTURE AND MIDDLEWARE

SQLView places itself between middleware (e.g., ODBC) and the client application, functioning as "upper middleware." It establishes and manages multiple connections for applications, maintains multiple result sets for a connection, and moves data from an application user interface to the database and back. Figure 7.1 illustrates the architecture of a Proto-Gen+ client/server application using SQLView.

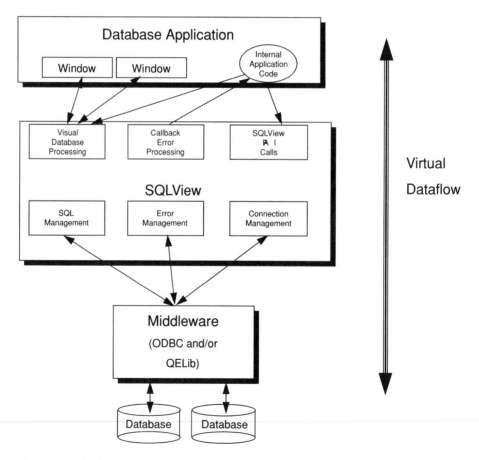

Figure 7.1 Architecture of client/server application using SQLView

SQLVIEW CONNECTIONS

SQLView establishes connections to the database for an application when the application first calls vwConnectView(), vwDoDriverLogon(), or vwConnect(). In most cases, SQLView only establishes one connection to each database for an individual application, although internally multiple connections may be maintained to support multiple database processes . . . however, this is outside the application's concern.

Once SQLView connects to the middleware driver, it creates the application driver environment object and places the handles it needs to access QELib or ODBC on this object.

Within the driver environment object, multiple database processes exist. A database process is activated when SQL statements are issued to the middleware component of the connection. SQLView separates SQL statements into two categories:

- data retrieval
- data change

Data retrieval (i.e., SELECT statements) is activated when a user clicks a button with an SQL find action associated with it or when a function call is made to vwExecSQL(). Data retrieval processes are referenced by a connection ID. It is important to note that a connection ID does not directly refer to the driver connection but rather to a database process occurring on that connection. From a connection ID, SQLView indirectly knows which driver environment object is involved.

By maintaining multiple data retrieval processes an application can, for example, browse multiple SQL SELECT statements concurrently, such as having two active database-connected dialogs accessing the same table and displaying different records for the user to update.

On each driver environment SQLView creates a special database process used for issuing "data change" SQL statements (e.g., INSERT, UPDATE, or DELETE statements). This database process is accessed by visual database processing for the Insert, Update, Delete, and custom SQL scripts, along with function calls to vwExecSQLChange(). When an application calls that function with a connection ID, the data retrieval process associated with the connection ID remains intact. This means that upon returning from a function call to vwExecSQLChange(), a subsequent call to vwFetchNext() or a GetNext with the same connection ID will retrieve the next record on the result set created by the dialog Find method.

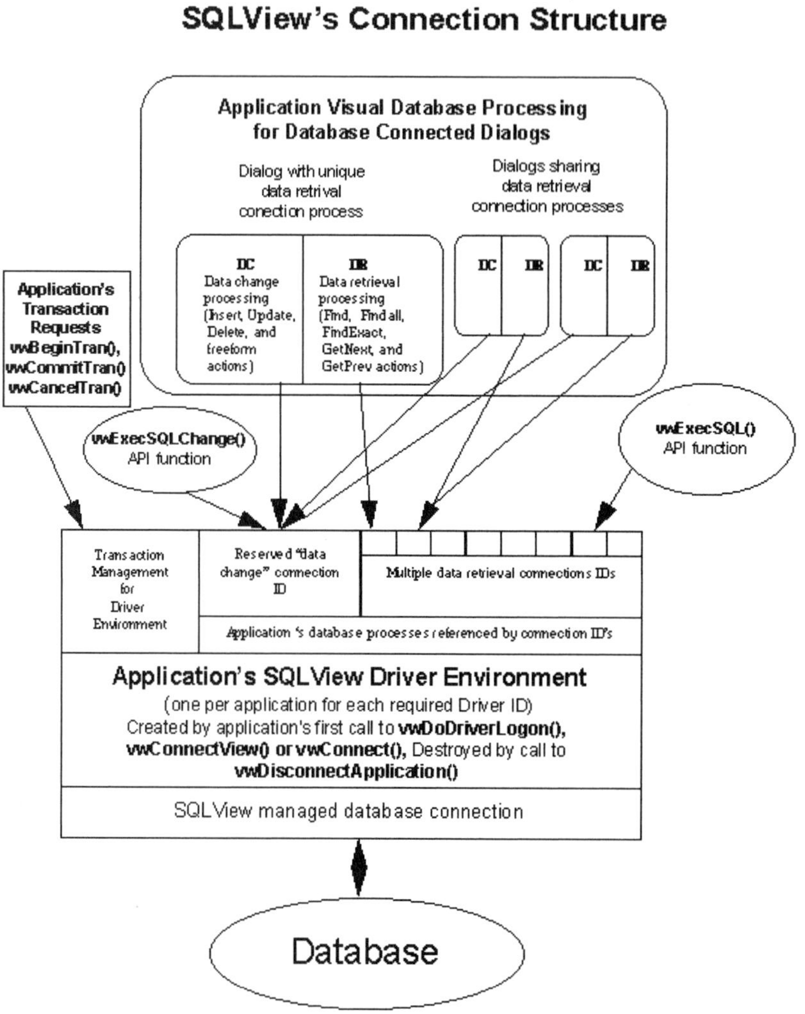

SQLView's Connection Structure

Application Visual Database Processing for Database Connected Dialogs

Dialog with unique data retrieval connection process

Dialogs sharing data retrieval connection processes

DC Data change processing (Insert, Update, Delete, and freeform actions)

DR Data retrieval processing (Find, Findall, FindExact, GetNext, and GetPrev actions)

DC DR DC DR

Application's Transaction Requests vwBeginTran(), vwCommitTran() vwCancelTran()

vwExecSQLChange() API function

vwExecSQL() API function

Transaction Management for Driver Environment

Reserved "data change" connection ID

Multiple data retrieval connections IDs

Application's database processes referenced by connection ID's

Application's SQLView Driver Environment

(one per application for each required Driver ID)
Created by application's first call to **vwDoDriverLogon()**,
vwConnectView() or **vwConnect()**, Destroyed by call to
vwDisconnectApplication()

SQLView managed database connection

Database

Figure 7.2 SQLView's connection structure

Figure 7.2 illustrates the database processes that are created and utilized on behalf of an application program.

For SQLView visual database processing, each database-connected dialog or view has a connection ID, which is used for data retrieval processes. The connection ID is associated with a view when vwConnectView() is called after dialog creation. A connected view may share or require distinct connection IDs, depending on the Boolean parameter to the function call.

By default, ProtoGen+ generates this function call for sharing of connection processes among dialogs. The function call can be changed within the code to request distinct connection identifiers. Dialogs with distinct connection identifiers will not overstep each other's data retrieval processes (e.g., find actions). For visual database processing that changes the database (e.g., Insert, Update, Delete, or custom SQL script actions), the visual database processor will execute these statements on the reserved "database change" connection ID for the driver environment. A call to the SQLView API function vwExecSQLChange() will also use this reserved connection ID. It is not necessary to know this connection ID in order to call this function. A call to this function with any valid connection ID referencing the driver environment will direct the supplied SQL statement to the reserved "data change" connection ID.

ESTABLISHING CONNECTIONS

A file in the Windows directory—SQLVIEW.INI—contains the information needed by SQLView to establish a database connection. Each entry in this file is referenced by a driver ID, key-coded by number to refer either to QELib or ODBC database sources.

USING SQLVIEW IN VIEWPAINT

In Chapter 5, we discussed the ViewPaint component of the ProtoGen+ environment. In this section we'll briefly look at how SQLView is used through ViewPaint.

Following the enabling of SQLView within ViewPaint (from a menu choice), a new dialog resource is created, as described in Chapter 5. In the client area of the new view, the right mouse button is then clicked to provide the developer with a floating menu, from which Edit View SQL Script can be selected.

Figure 7.3 illustrates the dialog of the Snap Table feature, from which database forms are created.

Figure 7.4 illustrates the resulting database form.

The database form can then be tested as a live dialog. Within the test environment, a developer's message box will appear in which the SQL statements that are being built can be viewed (these don't appear in the final application).

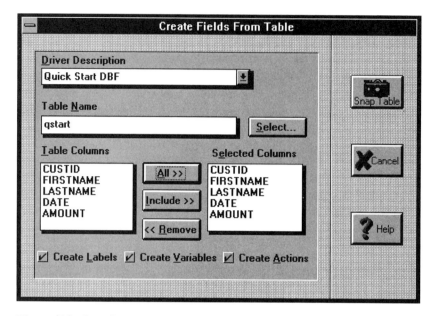

Figure 7.3 Creating a database form using Snap Table in ViewPaint

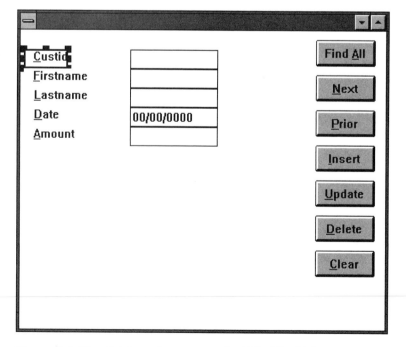

Figure 7.4 The database form created within ViewPaint

Figure 7.5 SQLView Actions selection dialog

For example, assume the developer wishes to include a "find exact" operation (e.g., an SQL SELECT statement with a WHERE clause that has some predicate that must be matched for rows to be retrieved). Figure 7.5 illustrates the dialog box (SQLView Actions) from which the "find exact" operation can be selected.

Choosing "find exact" will bring up a dialog from which the column for the WHERE clause can be selected (Figure 7.6).

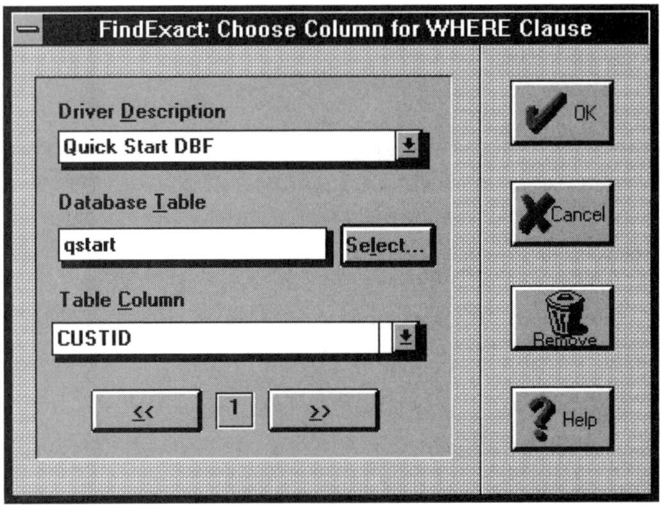

Figure 7.6 Selecting a column for the WHERE clause of FindExact

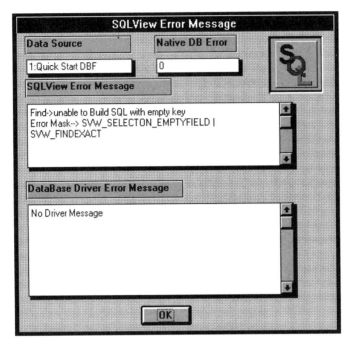

Figure 7.7 SQLView Error Message dialog box

ERROR DISPLAYS

SQLView has a developer error screen, which can be turned on and shut off through the SQLView Driver Manager in the ProtoGen+ program group on Windows. Figure 7.7 illustrates a resulting SQLView Error Message dialog box.

The dialog displays errors that SQLView encounters as it processes database actions. In order for an application to receive this information at run time it must register an SQLView error procedure when it calls the vwConnectView() function.

SQLVIEW METHODS

SQLView methods are ProtoView field string and view string, which SQLView uses to process its database-related tasks during the ProtoView Screen Management process. The methods are designed to be simple yet powerful enough to allow a developer to code information for complex SQL transactions.

There are two ways in which SQLView methods can be assigned to ProtoView controls. The SQLView/ViewPaint interface, as described above, is the easiest method, in effect parallel with the assigning of ProtoView Screen Manager controls while designing with ViewPaint. Alternatively, SQLView can be supplied with the method at run time using vwSetFieldString() and vwSetViewString().

The @VWFLD method links a database server connection, database table, and database column to a dialog field control. By assigning this method at run time, subsequent database actions involving this field's assigned column(s) will use the contents of this string to build SQL statements and return data to the field from the database.

The @VWFLD method takes a single argument (referred to as a "source argument") and consists of one or many source atoms of the form DriverId:TableName:ColumnName. DriverId is a specific database driver stored in the SQLVIEW.INI file (discussed above), while the names of the table and column identify a given column in a specific file. For example:

```
@VWFLD(0:CUSTOMERS.ZIP)
```

Alternatively, tables can be joined (linked) within the method, as in:

```
@VWFLD(0:CUSTOMERS:ZIP+0:ZIPCODES.ZIP)
```

In the second example, the field containing this method will be a join field based on zip code. SQLView will build SQL statements using join fields.

ATTACHING DATABASE ACTIONS TO PUSHBUTTONS, BITMAPS, AND ICONS

SQLView uses the @VWACTION method to attach database actions to pushbutton, bitmap, or icon controls. This method takes two arguments: the action and the source argument.

The action argument can be Insert, Update, Delete, FindExact, FindLike, FindAll, GetPrev, or GetNext. For each action specified, the source arguments and their component source atoms have different semantic meanings. These are discussed below.

The Insert Method

For an insert action, SQLView uses the source atoms in the source argument to issue an INSERT SQL statement for each table specified in the component source atoms. For example, a dialog may have the following SQLView methods:

```
Field 1  @VWFLD(0:CUST:ACCTNO+0:LOAN:LOANNUM)
Field 2  @VWFLD(0:CUST:NAME)
Field 3  @VWFLD(0:CUST:ADDRESS)
Field 4  @VWFLD(0:LOAN:LOANRATE)
Field 5  @VWFLD(0:LOAN:AMOUNT)
Button 1 @VWACTION (INSERT, 0:CUST:NULL+0:LOAN:NULL)
```

In accordance with the above dialog, when the application user clicks Button 1, SQLView will build and issue the following SQL statement to the dialog connection through driver 0:

- INSERT INTO CUST (ACCTNO, NAME, ADDRESS) VALUES (Field1, Field2, Field3)

- INSERT INTO LOAN (LOANNUM, LOANDATE, AMOUNT) VALUES (FIELD1, FIELD4, FIELD5)

SQLView will gather the field values from the appropriate control and insert them into the SQL statements. SQLView only uses the driver ID and table name components of each source atom in an add action method. The driver ID is used to determine where the SQL statement is sent. The table name is used in building the INSERT SQL statement. The column is extra information and by convention is best set to "NULL." Using View-Paint (Chapter 5) to create an insert button automatically ensures that this method is assigned correctly.

The Update Method

For an update action, SQLView uses the source atoms in the source argument to issue an UPDATE SQL statement for each table specified in the component source atoms and builds a WHERE clause for each column. Consider a dialog with the following SQLView methods:

```
Field 1  @VWFLD(0:CUST:ACCTNO+0:LOAN:LOANNUM)
Field 2  @VWFLD(0:CUST:NAME)
Field 3  @VWFLD(0:CUST:ADDRESS)
Field 4  @VWFLD(0:LOAN:LOANRATE)
Field 5  @VWFLD(0:LOAN:AMOUNT)
Button 1 @VWACTION (UPDATE, 0:CUST:ACCTNO+0:LOAN:LOANNUM)
```

When the user clicks Button 1, SQLView will build and issue the following SQL UPDATE statements to the dialog connection through driver 0:

- ```
  UPDATE CUST SET NAME = Field2, ADDRESS = Field3
  WHERE ACCTNO = Field1
  ```

- ```
  UPDATE LOAN SET LOANDATE = Field4, AMOUNT = Field5
  WHERE LOANNUM = Field1
  ```

In the above example, SQLView has used the column component of each source atom to build a WHERE clause. The developer can choose any column, but in most cases it makes sense to choose a unique key column for the source atom to force the UPDATE to affect only one record. If more than one record is affected by an update action, a message is sent through the dialog's registered SQLView callback error procedure (see Chapter 6 for a discussion of callbacks). The application can choose to either handle or ignore this message.

The Delete Method

For a delete action, SQLView uses the source atoms in the source argument to issue a DELETE SQL statement for each table specified in the component source atoms and builds a WHERE clause for each column. Again, consider the following dialog (here, the Button @VWACTION is different from those assigned in the above examples):

```
Field 1   @VWFLD(0:CUST:ACCTNO+0:LOAN:LOANNUM)
Field 2   @VWFLD(0:CUST:NAME)
Field 3   @VWFLD(0:CUST:ADDRESS)
Field 4   @VWFLD(0:LOAN:LOANRATE)
Field 5   @VWFLD(0:LOAN:AMOUNT)
Button 1 @VWACTION (DELETE, 0:CUST:NULL+0:LOAN:NULL)
```

Clicking Button 1 will cause SQLView to build and issue the following SQL delete statements to the dialog connection through driver 0:

- ```
  DELETE CUST WHERE ACCTNO = Field1 AND NAME = Field2
  AND ADDRESS = Field3
  ```

- ```
  DELETE LOAN WHERE LOANNUM = Field1 AND LOANDATE = Field4
  AND AMOUNT = Field5
  ```

The DELETE...WHERE statement spans every linked column for each table in the @VWACTION method source argument. In applications this implicitly requires that a user has found a record before that record can be deleted, or at least the exact values of every linked column on the dialog are known. For this source argument, the column components are extraneous and should be set to "NULL."

The FINDEXACT and FINDLIKE Methods

For a find action, SQLView uses the source atoms in the source argument to issue a SELECT SQL statement for each driver specified in the component source atoms and builds a WHERE clause for each column equal or similar to its field value. It then fills out the WHERE clause for every join field involving this driver. For example:

```
Field 1  @VWFLD(0:CUST:ACCTNO+0:LOAN:LOANNUM)
Field 2  @VWFLD(0:CUST:NAME)
Field 3  @VWFLD(0:CUST:ADDRESS)
Field 4  @VWFLD(0:LOAN:LOANRATE)
Field 5  @VWFLD(0:LOAN:AMOUNT)
Button 1 @VWACTION (FINDEXACT, 0:CUST:ACCTNO)
```

Clicking Button 1 will cause SQLView to build and issue the following SQL SELECT statement to the dialog connection through driver 0:

- SELECT CUST.ACCTNO, CUST.NAME, CUST.ADDRESS, LOAN.LOANDATE,
  LOAN.AMOUNT
  FROM CUST, LOAN
  WHERE CUST.ACCTNO = Field1 AND CUST.ACCTNO = LOAN.LOANNUM

FINDLIKE is implemented by placing a LIKE in the SELECT statement's WHERE clause. Since LIKE tends to vary from one DBMS to another, the exact specifics of a given back-end server should be identified to ensure predictable results.

The FINDALL Method

The FINDALL Method is used to retrieve all records in the table designated in the first source atom. For multiple source arguments SQLView will fill out the WHERE clause with the linked join fields and the FROM clause will contain both tables. For example:

```
Field 1   @VWFLD(0:CUST:ACCTNO+0:LOAN:LOANNUM)
Field 2   @VWFLD(0:CUST:NAME)
Field 3   @VWFLD(0:CUST:ADDRESS)
Field 4   @VWFLD(0:LOAN:LOANRATE)
Field 5   @VWFLD(0:LOAN:AMOUNT)
Button 1 @VWACTION (FINDALL, 0:CUST:NULL)
Button 2 @VWACTION (FINDALL, 0:CUST:NULL+0:LOAN:NULL)
```

Clicking Button 1 will cause SQLView to build and issue the following SQL statement:

- `SELECT CUST.ACCTNO, CUST.NAME, CUST.ADDRESS, FROM CUST`

Button 2 activation will cause the following SQL statement to be created and issued:

- `SELECT CUST.ACCTNO, CUST.NAME, CUST.ADDRESS, LOAN.LOANDATE,`
  `LOAN.LOANAMOUNT`
  `FROM CUST, LOAN`
  `WHERE CUST.ACCTNO = LOAN.LOANNUM`

OTHER METHODS

There are other SQLView methods that are used, including:

- @VWSQL allows customization of action buttons to access stored procedures or issue developer-defined SQL scripts. SQLView allows parameters to be placed in an SQL script using the @ character. When SQLView processes an SQL script, it will search the script and resolve the parameters denoted by @. The ProtoView function vwSetSQLVar() makes it possible to attach an SQL Var to a ProtoView control. Within an SQL script an @SQLVARNAME will be resolved to the field value at script activation. By assigning data elements to database-connected controls in ProtoGen+ the code generators will generate the vwSetSQLVar calls, setting the application and SQL variable to the name supplied.

- @VWCLEAR, when placed on a pvButton, pvBitmap, or pvIcon control, will clear the values from the controls containing the @VWFLD method within the view. There are no arguments for this method.

- @VWCONNID is a view method used by SQLView to establish connections for the view to its appropriate data sources. When the function call vwConnectView() is made, SQLView attempts to establish or find an existing connection to the drivers contained in this method's arguments. The arguments are a list of driver IDs, as defined in the SQLVIEW.INI file, separated by commas.

SQLVIEW AND CONTROLS

SQLView requires applications to use the ProtoView Screen Manager, which was discussed in the previous chapter. SQLView is also designed to work with the ProtoView WinControl Library (discussed in the next chapter) set of custom controls as well as the standard Windows Edit, Combobox, and Listbox controls. It also allows the Button, pvBitmap, and pvIcon controls to trigger predefined and custom SQL actions.

For representing data, it is a general rule to use a control that correlates to the data type of the column. For example, if the column contains date values, the pvDate control should be used. Currency values require the use of pvCurrency controls, and so on.

It is possible to provide the field methods (discussed in the previous sections) at run time for SQLView by calling the ProtoView function vwSetFieldString(), although it is easier and more efficient to supply this information at resource compile time by storing the information in the dialog file. By using SQLView and ViewPaint developers can build Database Connected Dialogs (DCDs), which are dialogs containing the proper SQL method information to enable SQLView to connect the dialog to its data source when the SQLView API functions vwConnectView() or vwConnectCopy() are called after view creation. In order for these functions to complete correctly, an @VWCONNID view method must be associated with the view. When using ViewPaint to set up DCDs, the @VWCONNID method is automatically calculated and placed on the dialog. This information can also be provided by directly placing the @VWCONNID method on the view using ViewPaint.

The Database Server combobox allows selection of the appropriate database driver ID as described in the SQLVIEW.INI file. Upon selection of a database, SQLView will attempt to establish the connection. If successful, the Select... button for the database table selection will become enabled. If the table is selected, SQLView will open the table and display the column selections in the Table Column combobox.

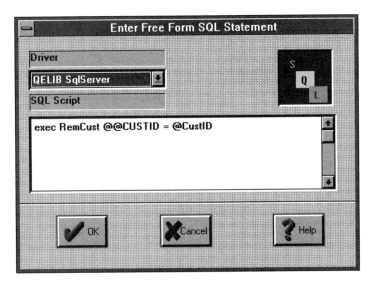

Figure 7.8 Building a custom SQL script for an action control

If SQLView isn't able to gather the table or column information due to connection problems, the table and column fields can be edited to input the appropriate information. The correct @VWFLD method will be associated with the control and stored in the dialog file, although test mode will likely not be able to connect this dialog until the connection problem is diagnosed and corrected.

LINKING ACTION CONTROLS TO SQL SCRIPTS

Within ViewPaint, action controls can be associated with database actions (SQL scripts). Using basically the same constructs as adding buttons to a dialog (discussed earlier in this chapter) in ViewPaint, a "Free-Form SQL Script" can be selected, as illustrated in Figure 7.8.

The dialog allows input of a custom SQL script to be issued to the selected data source upon activation of the related control. In the above example, SQLView will resolve the custom SQL script to "exec RemCust @CustID = 12345" (the data value contained in the control on the view with the SQLVar "CustID" associated with it through the function call vwSetSQLVar).

A custom script is useful for accessing database server stored procedures.

SUMMARY

In this chapter, we looked at the database side of the ProtoGen+ environment. In the next chapter, we'll briefly discuss the WinControl library facilities, completing our case study of the ProtoGen+ environment.

8

The ProtoView WinControl Library

INTRODUCTION

In this chapter, we'll briefly look at the WinControl library for Windows—a set of custom controls that augments the ProtoView Application Development Environment. These controls each perform special services and functions on behalf of application programs and dialog boxes, including data entry field formatting and validation and picture formatting. Other capabilities include a method script language for intelligent control creation without the need for program coding; utility functions to manipulate dates, times, numbers, and text; and color and other screen capabilities (e.g., 3D effects).

It should be noted that the ProtoView Screen Manager (Chapter 6) performs many of the functions and tasks described in this chapter, facilitating the open visual client/server development paradigm by alleviating many of the tedious development tasks previously performed by application developers.

WINCONTROL ARCHITECTURE

Open client/server computing means that a choice of environments should be available to application developers with respect to the tools they use. The WinControl library is designed to work in either of two environments:

- with the ProtoView Screen Manager (Chapter 6)
- with the Windows Dialog Manager

Even when the ProtoView Screen Manager isn't being used, the Win-Control library capabilities are available; it just requires more programming on the part of the application developers. Note that use with the ProtoView Screen Manager implies integration with the ViewPaint environment for visually developing applications (Chapter 5), but additionally the WinControl library provides a sophisticated message-based interface and function API that can be used to dynamically customize and control object behavior and characteristics.

WinControl messages are used to enable an application to interact directly with WinControl when it is necessary to accomplish specialized tasks. The predefined message types are:

- VW_SETFIELDSTRING
- VW_GETFIELDSTRING
- VW_EDITFIELD
- VW_APPTOSCR
- VW_SCRTOAPP

These are each discussed below.

VW_SETFIELDSTRING

This message is sent to a control to notify it of a change in the content of its data string. A field data string is a mechanism that allows a collection of data to be associated with a particular field control. By examining the contents of this data string at various message-processing points, a field control can carry out a variety of tasks without the need for application programming. The individual script commands within a field data string are called *methods*, because they are carried out in response to specific events occurring within the environment without having to be explicitly coded in the application logic.

Figure 8.1 illustrates an example of how a field string method can be set up for a pvBitmap control object, changing the appearance of a bitmap rapidly by using a timer.

```
#define BIT_TIMER        100
    BOOL bFlash;

    case WM_INITDIALOG :
        SetTimer(hWnd, BIT_TIMER, 500, NULL);
        bFlash = FALSE;
        break;

    case WM_TIMER :
        if(wParam == BIT_TIMER)
        {
            if(bFlash)
                SendMessage(hWndBitmap, VW_SETFIELDSTRING, 0,
                            (LPARAM)"@BITMAP(Flash.bmp)");
            else
                SendMessage(hWndBitmap, VW_SETFIELDSTRING, 0,
                            (LPARAM)"@BITMAP(Blank.bmp)");
            bFlash = ~bFlash;
        }
        break;
```

Figure 8.1 Using a message to dynamically change a field string method with WinControl

Note that when WinControl is used in conjunction with ProtoGen+ the process of selecting field methods and implementing them as field strings is entirely automated. The designer selects the options from choices in the ViewPaint Dialog Editor or types in custom methods. ViewPaint then takes care of saving the data strings in the application resources where they are compiled to binary form, and at run time they are automatically read in and passed to the field controls when the dialog window is created.

VW_GETFIELDSTRING

This message is used to retrieve the contents of a field's data string—for example, passing a buffer filled with the control's data string. The buffer can be manipulated to either add or remove field methods from the data string. After alteration, the field string can be reset again using VW_SETFIELDSTRING (above). Any new methods specified in the new field string immediately take effect when the control receives the VW_SETFIELDSTRING message.

VW_EDITFIELD

This message can be sent to a field control at various times to have the field validate its contents. If no error is found, VW_NOERROR is returned; otherwise, VW_ERROR is.

The type of validation performed varies with the different control classes. Each control has built-in, predefined validation capabilities plus any custom methods added through program control, and these are invoked in response to receiving the VW_EDITFIELD message. The most common events triggering VW_EDITFIELD processing are the exit of a field control focus and the termination of a dialog box or data entry form.

When the Screen Manager is present, these events automatically trigger VW_EDITFIELD processing. When the Screen Manager is not being used, it is the application's responsibility to send the VW_EDITFIELD message to perform the data validation.

WinControl takes one of several actions when an error in a field control's contents is detected. A warning message can be displayed, but the user can proceed to the next field if so desired; or the user will not be allowed to proceed to the next field. The parent window can also respond

```
static HWND hWndNum

case WM_INITDIALOG :
     hWndNum = GetDlgItem(hDlg, ID_NUMERIC);
     // Establish a range check for the field
     SendMessage(hWndNum, VW_SETFIELDSTRING, 0,
     (LPARAM)"@RNG(0, 100)  @MSG(Enter values between 0 and 100.)");
     break;

case WM_COMMAND :
if((wParam == ID_NUMERIC) && (HIWORD(lParam) == EN_KILLFOCUS))
{
     // Allow focus to change if there was no error
     if(VW_NOERROR == SendMessage(hWndNum, VW_EDITFIELD, 0, 0))
          SetFocus(GetDlgItem(GetNextDlgID(hDlg)));
     else
     // Otherwise keep the focus at the current control
          SetFocus(hWndNum);
}
break;
```

Figure 8.2 Using the VW_EDITFIELD (example)

to the error condition in a custom fashion if necessary because WinControl notifies it with a VW_ERRORSET message.

Figure 8.2 illustrates an example of setting up a field string for a pvNumeric control object to be invoked upon receipt of the VW_EDITFIELD message.

VW_APPTOSCR and VW_SCRTOAPP

The last two types of messages perform data conversion to and from the screen, respectively. Each WinControl class is capable of converting screen data (in character format) into one of several possible internal data types (integer, character string, etc.).

As has been noted earlier, it is the responsibility of the designer to ensure that the data type of the variable associated with a control agrees

```
char StringField[80];
LONG LongField;
struct tm DateField;

case WM_INITDIALOG :
    // Convert data from application to screen
    SendDlgItemMessage(hDlg, VW_APPTOSCR, ID_STRINGFIELD, 0,
        (LPARAM)(LPSTR)StringField);
    SendDlgItemMessage(hDlg, VW_APPTOSCR, ID_LONGFIELD, 0,
        (LPARAM)(LPSTR)&LongField);
    SendDlgItemMessage(hDlg, VW_APPTOSCR, ID_DATEFIELD, 0,
        (LPARAM)(LPSTR)&DateField);
    break;

case WM_COMMAND :
if(wParam == IDOK)
{
    // Convert data from screen to application
    SendDlgItemMessage(hDlg, VW_SCRTOAPP, ID_STRINGFIELD, 0,
        (LPARAM)(LPSTR)StringField);
    SendDlgItemMessage(hDlg, VW_SCRTOAPP, ID_LONGFIELD, 0,
        (LPARAM)(LPSTR)&LongField);
    SendDlgItemMessage(hDlg, VW_SCRTOAPP, ID_DATEFIELD, 0,
        (LPARAM)(LPSTR)&DateField);
}
break;
```

Figure 8.3 Converting data to and from the screen

with the data type style given to the control; otherwise, unpredictable behavior or protection faults may occur. Using the ProtoGen+ code generator to produce the application helps to ensure the compatibility.

Figure 8.3 shows an example of using these two messages.

VALIDATION WITH WINCONTROL

The WinControl library contains built-in validation methods for the data entered into many field control classes. These methods are easiest to implement and most effective when used in conjunction with ProtoGen+, but they can also be utilized directly from an application program.

Upon receipt of a VW_EDITFIELD message, WinControl controls execute validation methods. The message is sent automatically by the ProtoView Screen Management Facility whenever the user attempts to leave a field, by use of either the mouse or the keyboard. It is also sent when the vwEditField() or vwEditView() functions are called. Application programs

```
case WM_COMMAND :
if((wParam == IDOK)
{     // Allow dialog to close only if there was no error
      if(VW_ERROR== SendDlgItemMessage(hWndNum, ID_FIRSTNAME,
              VW_EDITFIELD, 0, 0))
          return 0;
      if(VW_ERROR == SendDlgItemMessage(hWndNum, ID_LASTNAME,
              VW_EDITFIELD, 0, 0))
          return 0;
      if(VW_ERROR == SendDlgItemMessage(hWndNum, ID_ADDRESS,
              VW_EDITFIELD, 0, 0))
          return 0;
      if(VW_ERROR == SendDlgItemMessage(hWndNum, ID_CITY,
              VW_EDITFIELD, 0, 0))
          return 0;
      if(VW_ERROR == SendDlgItemMessage(hWndNum, ID_STATE
              VW_EDITFIELD, 0, 0))
          return 0;
      if(VW_ERROR == SendDlgItemMessage(hWndNum, ID_ZIPCODE
              VW_EDITFIELD, 0, 0))
          return 0;
} break;
```

Figure 8.4 Using the VW_EDITFIELD message for validation

can also send this message to a WinControl object at any time to perform editing and validation of the field contents.

Figure 8.4 illustrates how field editing can take place from a dialog procedure when the OK pushbutton has been activated. If any of the VW_EDITFIELD messages have returned VW_ERROR, the dialog is *not* allowed to close.

WinControl manages data validation through a library function, vwValidate(). This can perform mandatory, choice, range, and table lookup validation on a variety of data types and can be called either from application programs or by field controls to validate a data item. If the validation is successful, the function returns TRUE; otherwise, it returns FALSE.

Error handling is also initiated by the vwValidate() function, beginning with sending a notification message (VW_ERRORSET) to the parent window of the field in error. The parent window, upon receiving this message, can invoke error handling itself or can let default error handling take place. When processing has been completed, a return code of VW-ERROR_PROCESSED is returned.

SUMMARY

This chapter has presented a brief overview of the WinControl library facilities in the ProtoGen+ environment. Again, as mentioned previously, the complete set of ProtoGen+ documentation provides much greater detail with respect to these capabilities. Additionally, the staff at ProtoView Development Corporation should be contacted for product information and other details about the facilities discussed.

PART III

Case Study 2

9

Overview of db-UIM/X

INTRODUCTION

db-UIM/X is an interactive tool through which the developer can create OSF/Motif user interfaces quickly and easily. All phases of interface development—layout, behavior specification, testing, refinement, and code generation—are handled from within db-UIM/X. One of the advantages of using db-UIM/X as compared with traditional development environments is that the time-consuming compile/link/debug cycles are not required to design, develop, "tweak," and adjust applications during the life cycle.

This chapter introduces the db-UIM/X environment and provides a foundation for discussion in the subsequent chapters of the book.

PROJECTS

A project usually consists of one or more interfaces and, sometimes, one or more palettes. In db-UIM/X the developer can save these interfaces and/or palettes individually or, if desired, together in a *project*. When the developer chooses to work with projects, all phases of the application—from design to generation of the executable—can be accomplished entirely within db-UIM/X. Projects can be refined by using the Project

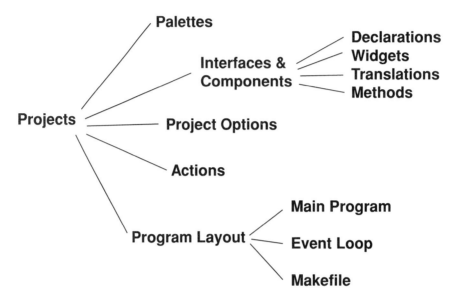

Figure 9.1 Components of a db-UIM/X project

Window, and individual interfaces can be polished by using the Browser. Figure 9.1 illustrates the components of a db-UIM/X project.

Some of the benefits of working with projects include:

- saving all interfaces and/or palettes in one operation
- loading all interfaces and/or palettes into db-UIM/X by opening an existing project
- generating code for all interfaces in one operation
- generating automatically an application's main program and make-file
- saving the current options for db-UIM/X as part of the project

DESIGNING THE INTERFACE LAYOUT

The first phase of interface development is typically the layout, or the look of the application. Using db-UIM/X the designer/developer can draw the interface with a direct manipulation WYSIWYG (What You See Is What You Get) editor. The designer can also use db-UIM/X to build palettes of *reusable* interface components.

db-UIM/X supports all of OSF/Motif: every shell, widget, gadget, convenience dialog, and resource; all of these can be used to build user interfaces.

The layout can be refined by setting the properties and resources of the widgets that comprise an interface. db-UIM/X has a wide range of interactive editing operations and covers all OSF/Motif functions. The designer can use direct manipulation to edit the individual widgets and widget hierarchies.

ATTACHING C CODE

The second phase of interface development typically is *behavior specification*—the *feel* of the application. Behavior specification involves setting all of the dynamic elements of the interface. Specifying and testing the behavior accounts for approximately 60–80 percent of the entire user interface development time.

By using db-UIM/X the developer can specify user-interface behavior with a suite of components.

- Callbacks: These are actions that occur when the user presses buttons, moves scroll bars, or chooses menu entries.

- Application window behavior: These are actions that occur in the application window (for example, in a drawing program the area where a user draws and makes circles is the application window). The user must specify what the application should do when he or she presses the mouse button, drags the mouse, and so on.

- Dynamic elements of the initial state: These are the elements that dynamically depend on the state of the application; for example, a radio button in a dialog box may be set differently each time the dialog box is popped up.

These are each discussed below.

Specifying Callbacks

Callbacks are specified by entering their application function calls in C. The developer has access to all callback arguments along with all Xm, Xt, and X function calls. These calls are linked in with the development version of db-UIM/X. Additionally, calls can be made to the developer's own widgets. These also can be linked in with db-UIM/X.

To facilitate specifying behavior, db-UIM/X is equipped with the *Ux Convenience Library*. The library performs tasks such as converting resources, allocating colormap entries, automatically managing children of dialog shells, and handling special cases of geometry management. The library performs substantial error checking, notification, and recovery. By using the Ux Convenience Library, the developer doesn't have to learn OSF/Motif function library and programming style.

Specifying Application Window Behavior

Application window behavior is specified through the use of translation, action, and event tables. These enable the developer to graphically specify events and tie them to C code actions. In addition to graphically selecting common events, the developer can also choose any Toolkit event.

Once a translation table has been defined, the developer can then customize the behavior of existing widgets by applying the table to them. db-UIM/X supports all three Toolkit modes of modifying widget behavior: augment, override, and replace (e.g., the developer can add behavior to support the drawing functions of an application, modify behavior to add double-click actions to buttons, or replace behavior of the widgets with drag-and-drop functions).

Dynamic Initial State

When popping up an interface, typically 15–20 percent of the resources in most interfaces depend on the state of the application at any given time. Settings that change when a new file is loaded or settings that depend on command-line arguments are examples. db-UIM/X permits the developer to specify and test such *parametric user interfaces*. To build a parametric user interface, the developer specifies a C expression as the initial value of any resource. That C expression is evaluated when the widget is created, both by db-UIM/X when building the interface and in the generated code. The C expression can be any legal C expression that returns the correct type: a function call with arguments, an application global variable, and so forth.

In addition to specifying parametric interfaces, db-UIM/X permits the developer to build reusable components. In db-UIM/X a reusable component is a top-level interface that is repeatedly used in other interfaces. The component can be an actual interface or can exist only as C code. A component can be instantiated within any other interface or manager widget.

Reusable components can act as easy and fast alternatives to building custom widgets, or as a means to enhance productivity across multiple projects. Parametric interfaces and components can contain anything that db-UIM/X can build, including widget hierarchies and translation tables.

To build a reusable parametric component, the developer specifies arguments to the function call that creates it. The arguments may, in turn, be used in the C expression in the resource slots of any widget in the component. Components can be either top-level interfaces (e.g., interfaces with a Shell widget) or children deep in the widget hierarchy.

db-UIM/X supports multiple instances of parametric interfaces and reusable components within an application, each with a separate context. This ensures that reusability is a practical reality.

db-UIM/X also supports methods for both interfaces and components. Methods provide the means by which application software can address—or submit requests to—an interface; for example, among other functions, methods provide a means of updating interfaces after changes have been made to data.

SETTING APPLICATION DEFAULTS

db-UIM/X can be configured by setting the *Application Defaults*, using *resources*. Changing the value associated with a resource permits the developer to configure db-UIM/X for a variety of operating environments and user preferences.

Application Defaults can be set system-wide (for all users), for a single user, or for a single instance of db-UIM/X.

TESTING AND REFINING INTERFACES

As a part of the creation process, testing and refining the user interface is important to the overall development/deployment life cycle. db-UIM/X contains a built-in C Interpreter, which permits the developer to build, modify, and test a user interface with the underlying application running, but without the compile/link/debug cycle.

The db-UIM/X C Interpreter can mix compiled and interpreted code. It can modify compiled global variables and pass the address of an interpreted routine into a compiled routine for dereferencing and execution. Because the developer can link the compiled application code with db-UIM/X, db-UIM/X enables the building and testing of the user interface with the application needed to drive it.

db-UIM/X supports an incremental approach to software development, something very important for open client/server applications and systems. The C Interpreter can be used to rapidly develop interfaces and, once they have been validated, the interfaces can be compiled individually for performance. db-UIM/X also supports a modular approach to development, enabling the entry of interface C code into callbacks and completely separating the user interface from its application code. As was discussed in Chapter 2, application partitioning models for next-generation client/server architecture typically demand a separation of user interface from business/application logic.

GENERATING CODE

Once an interface has been validated (i.e., it is "correct" and the developer is satisfied), db-UIM/X generates portable code in C to a variety of different standards. It also can generate C++ code or a combination of either UIL and C or UIL and C++.

db-UIM/X also generates a resource file for each interface in which at least one widget has a property source set to public. End users can therefore customize the widget by changing that property's value. By setting widget property sources to private or public, the developer can control how much or how little of the user interface can be customized by the user.

Additionally, applications can be built that can be customized for the international market. Calls to the message catalog functions to specify initial values for labels and fonts, changing message lengths, and other by-location resources can be part of the generated environment.

OTHER CAPABILITIES

In some applications there is a requirement to handle other data sources besides mouse and keyboard inputs. Many financial applications, for example, use "live market data feeds" in which real-time quotes for securities instruments need to be processed. Many embedded applications require being able to accept data from physical input devices (e.g., aircraft instruments). db-UIM/X gives the developer full access to the event loop so requirements such as those listed above can be met.

In many client/server environments that involve migration from legacy applications[1] one of the first steps is adding a new user interface to existing applications. db-UIM/X supports this phased migration paradigm in two ways—one for when the goal is to avoid modifying the application and the other for when the application can be modified but not restructured. In effect, db-UIM/X supports a phased, incremental migration/transition approach as new technologies are infused into the organization.

SOFTBENCH INTERACTION

Hewlett-Packard's SoftBench[2] (a window-based interface to software development tools and utilities) can include db-UIM/X in the supported tool suite. The details of this are beyond the scope of this book, but information about including db-UIM/X into an open integrated development environment under SoftBench can be found in *The db-UIM/X Developer's Guide*, Appendix C.

SUMMARY

This chapter has presented a brief overview of the db-UIM/X environment. The following chapters will go into more detail about most of the items discussed in this chapter. For further details, the db-UIM/X documentation set, available from Bluestone, should be consulted.

ENDNOTES

1. Systems migration is discussed in A. Simon, *Systems Migration: The Complete Reference* (New York: Van Nostrand Reinhold/Intertext, 1992), and S. Shaffer and A. Simon, *Transitioning to Open Systems* (San Mateo, CA: Morgan Kaufmann, in press).

2. SoftBench is discussed in A. Simon, *The Integrated CASE Tools Handbook* (New York: Van Nostrand Reinhold/Intertext, 1993).

10

Interacting with db-UIM/X

INTRODUCTION

This chapter discusses the basic concepts of how the developer interacts with db-UIM/X, including:

- starting db-UIM/X
- starting db-UIM/X with alternative interfaces and files
- starting db-UIM/X with user palettes
- common window buttons
- using the text editor
- saving work
- resetting db-UIM/X
- exiting db-UIM/X
- the project window menu bar
- pop-up menus
- project window menus in test mode

As in our discussion of ProtoView, the material in this chapter is intended to provide the reader, particularly someone who has never worked with client/server visual development tools, with a "test drive" of the distinctions between traditional 3GL programming and "modern" software development techniques. Subsequent chapters will discuss the functionality of many of these areas in more detail.

STARTING DB-UIM/X

The steps in starting a db-UIM/X session are listed below:

1. Start the X Window System.

2. Open a terminal window.

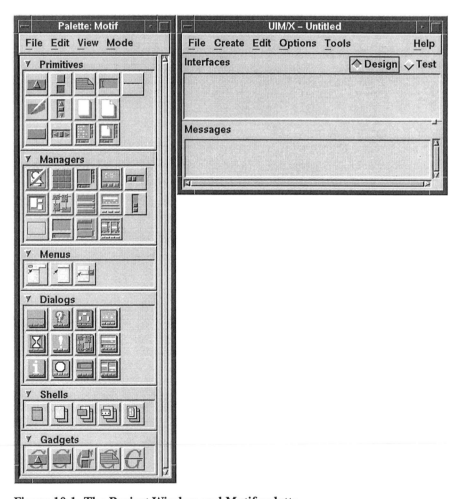

Figure 10.1 The Project Window and Motif palette

3. At the UNIX prompt, start db-UIM/X by entering:

    dbuimx & <ENTER> *

4. After the start-up screens (copyright notice, etc.) the db-UIM/X
    Project Window (Figure 10.1) appears, and the developer can then
    begin working with db-UIM/X.

5. The terminal window should then be iconified (turned into an
    icon).

THE PROJECT WINDOW

The Project Window comprises the following areas (shown in Figure
10.2):

Area	Description
Title Bar	Displays the project title
Menu Bar	Contains the pull-down menus
Design/Test	Displays the current operating mode
Interfaces Area	Displays icons representing each interface in the project
Messages	Displays system error and status messages

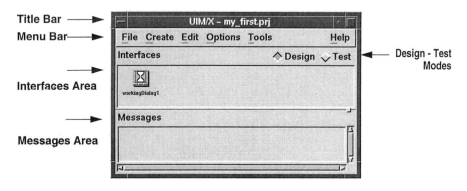

Figure 10.2 The Project Window

---

* Note that the PATH variable must provide the full path to the db-UIM/X executable to
use the command shown; if this is not the case, the full directory path must be part of the
command line, as in /usr/dbuimx2.6/bin/dbuimx & .

CHANGING THE OPERATING MODE

Design mode is the default operating mode for db-UIM/X; this mode allows the developer to interactively create and modify widgets to construct user interfaces.

By clicking the Test toggle button the mode is switched to Test mode, in which the application's interfaces can be tested without compiling.

While constructing interfaces, it is common to frequently toggle between the Design and Test modes; using the toggles enables the design/test cycle to be accomplished rapidly, as compared with traditional software development compile/link/debug cycles.

STARTING DB-UIM/X WITH ALTERNATIVE INTERFACES AND FILES

By default, db-UIM/X starts with an empty Project Window. As is common in most computer applications, it is often desirable to start the program with an existing project loaded. Or, by setting resources, db-UIM/X can be started in Test mode or with the Browser instead of the Project Window in the start-up interface.

Automatic project loading is accomplished by following the command with

```
-file file1.prj &
```

where file1.prj is the name of a project file. Once db-UIM/X is initialized, the project appears on the screen (Figure 10.3).

Alternatively, the Browser—a tool to view and edit the widget hierarchy—can be specified at start-up (the Browser is shown in Figure 10.4) by using a resource specification:

```
Dbuimx2_6*UxStartupInterface.value:browser
```

Starting in Test mode is accomplished by setting the value to "test." Note, however, that starting in Test mode means that the developer *cannot* toggle/change to Design mode.

Through command-line options and parameters (all discussed in the db-UIM/X documentation), the Browser can be started with a file, or Test

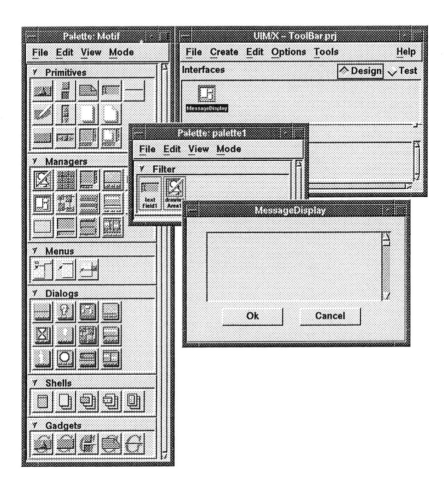

Figure 10.3 Starting db-UIM/X with a project

mode can be started with a file. Similarly, in addition to using the Motif
palette (shown in Figure 10.1), customized palettes can be loaded (see
Figure 10.5), again by using the resource settings:

```
Dbuimx2_6*UxStartingPalettes.value: palette_name
Dbuimx2_6*UxPalettePath.value: absolute_path_name
```

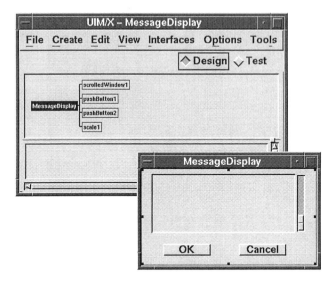

Figure 10.4 Starting db-UIM/X with the Browser and an interface

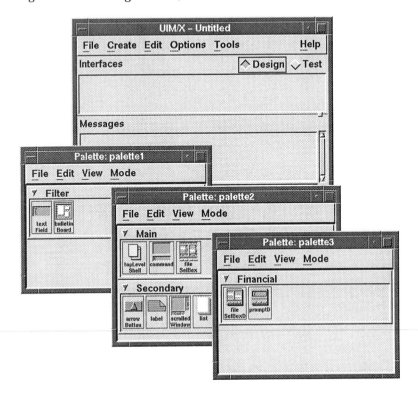

Figure 10.5 Starting db-UIM/X with user palettes

COMMON WINDOW BUTTONS

Many of db-UIM/X's windows have a common set of buttons (OK, Apply, and Cancel). Their behavior is described below.

Button Selection	Description
OK	Saves changes and closes the window
Apply	Saves changes *without* closing the window
Cancel	Closes the window *without* saving the changes

THE TEXT EDITOR

db-UIM/X contains a full-screen text editor. This is available in many places within db-UIM/X and is always denoted by a Text Editor (...) button beside the field that is to be edited. The button appears in the Action Table Editor, the Translation Table Editor, the Widget Property Editor, the Menu Editor, and the Declarations Editor.

Sometimes the full-screen text editor doesn't need to be opened. In cases where it is desirable to edit a text field, this is accomplished by pointing (via the mouse) into a field and typing into it; as long as the mouse pointer remains over it, typing can be done.

SAVING WORK

As is the case with most applications, work is saved via a SAVE command (specifically, SAVE PROJECT or SAVE PROJECT AS...). When code is generated for the first time, it is necessary to save the project again; this second save ensures that if the project is modified again, db-UIM/X will use the same path to save the code.

RESETTING DB-UIM/X

When working in db-UIM/X it is sometimes desirable to start over on a particular project or change and work on another project. This can be done by resetting db-UIM/X. All work (e.g., interfaces, palettes) must be saved prior to the reset. Alternatively, loading a new project will effect a reset operation.

THE PROJECT WINDOW'S MENU BAR

The Project Window's menu bar contains menus for File, Create, Edit, Options, Tools, and Help. These are described in the chart below.

Menu Selection	Description
File	Choices include opening, closing, and saving files; generating project code; showing and hiding interfaces and palettes.
Create	Allows creation of three types of top-level widgets: Shell, Manager, and Dialog. Additionally, palettes and subclasses can be created.
Edit	Editing options are selected (displaying the Action Table Editor, the Widget Browser, the Declarations Editor, the Methods Editor, or the Program Layout Editor).
Options	A number of developer-defined options can be set: grid defaults, code generation options, options for the Property Editor, and so on.
Tools	This menu permits selection of the C Interpreter, the Browser, the Property Editor, and can show or hide the Palette Area.
Help	"About" information (version number, etc.) and preliminary "Getting Started" information is obtained.

POP-UP MENUS

By pressing the Menu mouse button, pop-up menus can be accessed. For example, the Interfaces Area of the Project Window contains icons representing each interface in the project (Figure 10.6), and a pop-up menu can be accessed from which operations can be performed on those interfaces.

PROJECT WINDOW MENUS IN TEST MODE

Finally, many of the pull-down menus on the Project Window's menu bar function differently in Test mode than in Design mode (the examples in this chapter have focused on Design mode operations). For example,

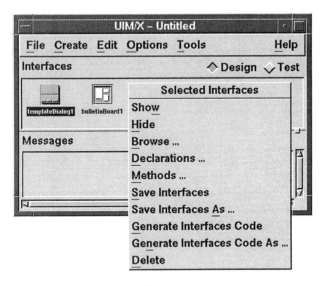

Figure 10.6 The Selected Interfaces pop-up menu

many of the Tools and Selected Interfaces pop-up menu choices are unavailable in Test mode, since they apply to designing . . . and no designing is done while in Test mode.

SUMMARY

This chapter has presented a brief overview of how the developer interacts with db-UIM/X. The next chapter will discuss, in more detail, how interfaces are built and how the user works with widgets.

11

Working with Widgets and Building Interfaces

INTRODUCTION

db-UIM/X allows developers to build user interfaces by assembling Motif widgets into a *widget hierarchy*. One widget is placed upon another to make a structure of parents and children. A child widget can be the parent of other widgets, and each widget is intended to perform a specific task.

In this chapter, we'll present an overview of working with widgets and building interfaces, leading into the discussions in the following chapters where we'll explore the open client/server aspects of db-UIM/X in more detail. While we will be reviewing the Motif widget set, it is important to note that other widgets and class libraries may be integrated into db-UIM/X. An example is a C++ class library called the Cross Platform Toolset, which provides for both Motif and MS-Windows application code generation.

INTERFACES AND SHELLS

The first widget in any widget hierarchy is a *top-level widget*. As a top-level widget interacts with the window manager, it must be assigned a Shell widget to manage the interaction. In db-UIM/X the developer can create these Shell widgets explicitly or let db-UIM/X assign them to widgets.

Shells that are created by the developer are referred to as *explicit Shells*, while *implicit Shells* are those assigned by db-UIM/X.

There are tradeoffs with respect to the use of the above two types of Shells that, as in any client/server development situation, must be considered by the developers and application architects. By assigning a Shell widget explicitly, the developer can control how the widget interacts with the window manager and, through the Property Editor, have access to all of the properties necessary to change the Shell's behavior when it interacts with the window manager. At the same time, implicit shells can be used automatically, but their properties cannot be accessed.

In db-UIM/X widgets are organized into five categories or classes (discussed below), and within a hierarchy they are related to each other as parent and child. The first widget of an interface (the top-level widget) has no parent, and all child widgets have one parent. Some widgets cannot have children, but, in general, every widget in the hierarchy (other than the top-level widget) has one and only one parent widget and is a child widget.

The types of widgets are listed below.

- Shell widgets
- Manager widgets
- Dialog widgets
- Primitive Widgets
- Gadgets

The Shell Widgets

The following Shell widgets—all of which function as top-level interfaces (never as children) and which permit dictating features to the window manager—are shown below.

Widget Name	Description
Application Shell	This is used for an application's primary top-level window (a subclass of the top-level Shell).
Dialog Shell	This is used for Dialog widgets (a subclass of the Transient Shell).

Widget Name	*Description*
Override Shell	Used mainly for pop-up menus—these completely bypass the window manager.
Top-Level Shell	Used for top-level widgets (other than the primary Application Window)—these can be manipulated and iconified by the window manager.
Transient Shell	Used for Dialog widgets—these can be manipulated by the window manager, but not separately iconified.

Manager Widgets

Manager widgets control their children in a particular fashion, according to the type of Manager created. Manager widgets can be top-level interfaces or the children of Shell or other Manager widgets.

The Manager widgets are shown below.

Widget Name	*Description*
Bulletin Board	This is a general layout widget, used as the foundation for *building dialogs*. It may arbitrarily have many children, and it imposes some constraints on the layout of children. It is typically used as a child of a Dialog Shell.
Command	This provides a command history, including a message area, an input region, a scrolling list of previous commands, and command buttons.
Drawing Area	This is a general layout widget. It may have many children and imposes no constraints on the layout of children.
File Selection Box	This provides a file selection mechanism, including a message area, a field for the directory mask, a scrolling list of file names, an editable input field for the selected file, and command buttons.

Widget Name	Description
Form	This is a layout widget. It may have many children and permits the developer to specify constraints on the location of children. It is typically used to ensure that a particular layout is proportionally maintained even when the user resizes the window.
Frame	This provides an etched or three-dimensional border decoration for its work-area child. It also supports one title child and generic children and imposes some constraints on its children.
Main Window	This is a layout widget that provides a standard layout for the primary window of an application and automatically manages its children, which may include a menu bar, a command window, a work region, and scroll bars.
Message Box	This provides a means to pass information to the user and includes a symbol, a message area, and command buttons.
Paned Window	This is a composite widget that lays out children in a vertical format, from top to bottom.
Row Column	A layout widget that may have many children, but forces them to appear in a matrix format with distinct rows and columns. It is used as the underlying widget for menu bars, pop-up menu panes, pull-down menus, and option menus.
Scale	This allows the user to select a value from a range of values by positioning a slider inside an elongated rectangular region; a scale may be either vertical or horizontal.
Scrolled Window	This is a layout widget that may have one child and be configured to provide scroll bars when the size of the child exceeds the size of the scrolled window.

Widget Name	*Description*
Selection Box	This provides a means for a user to make a selection from among a number of alternatives. It provides a message area, an editable field, a scrolling list of choices, and command buttons.

Dialog Widgets

Dialog widgets are a collection of widgets used for file selection or to display warning messages. Dialog widgets are top-level widgets and can never be child widgets, although they can be Instances of a Component. Dialog widgets include the following:

Widget Name	*Description*
Bulletin Board	This is typically used when building a custom dialog.
Error	This is a message box showing the Motif error symbol. It is typically used when displaying an error to the user.
File Selection Box	A file selection box is inside a Dialog Shell widget. It is typically used when requesting that the user select a file.
Form	Form is typically used when building a custom dialog that the user can resize.
Information	This is a message box showing the Motif information symbol. It is typically used to display information to the user.
Message Box	The message box is used to display a message to the user.
Prompt	The prompt is used to request input from the user.
Question	A message box showing a question symbol, typically used to request a Yes/No reply from the user.

Widget Name	Description
Selection Box	The selection box is used to permit the user to choose from a list of items.
Template	The template is used for constructing one's own dialogs.
Warning	A message box showing a warning symbol is typically used to display a warning to the user.
Working	A message box showing a "working" symbol indicates to the user that the application is processing.

Primitive Widgets

Primitive widgets are used to perform a variety of functions, such as providing an arrow for scrolling, a text field for entering data, and so on. The table below shows the available Primitive Widgets within db-UIM/X.

Widget Name	Description
Arrow Button	This button displays an arrow pointing up, down, left, or right, and it is used for much the same purpose as a pushbutton (described below).
Drawn Button	This is a button widget with functionality similar to a pushbutton, but with an empty widget window. The application provides the graphics to be displayed in the widget.
Label	A Label widget is used to display either text or pixmaps.
List	A List widget provides the capability to display a collection of text strings and to make selections from them.
Pushbutton	A Pushbutton widget contains a text label or pixmap, which is responsive to select and release events from the Select mouse button and is used to invoke actions.

Widget Name	*Description*
Scroll Bar	The scroll bar is used to implement scrolling in a scrolled window or in other windows. The scroll bar can be either vertical or horizontal. When creating a scroll bar from the pull-down or pop-up menus, the direction in which the scroll bar is drawn determines its horizontal or vertical properties.
Scrolled List	This is a scrolled window with a List widget work area.
Scrolled Text	This is a scrolled window with a Text widget work area.
Separator	A separator widget is used to separate child widgets in a Manager widget; various line types are available.
Text	A Text widget functions as a single-line or multiline text editor.
Text Field	This is a single-line text editor widget (with higher performance than the Text widget described above).
Toggle Button	This is a widget containing text or pixmap and an indicator box showing the current status of the widget. It is used to display and change the state of a binary variable.

Gadgets

Gadgets are somewhat less flexible than Primitive widgets (they have fewer resources associated with them), but they are more efficient. A Gadget must always be the child of a Manager or Dialog widget and can never be a Parent Widget.

Available gadgets are:

- Arrow Button
- Label
- Pushbutton
- Separator
- Toggle Button

CREATING WIDGETS

All widgets can be created from the Motif palette (Figure 10.1), the palette displayed by default with the Project Window at startup (unless otherwise specified). Within the Motif palette, the widget classes are arranged into categories.

- Primitives
- Dialogs
- Managers
- Shells
- Menus
- Gadgets

Additionally, widgets can be created from the Create pull-down menu of the Project Window or from the Selected Widgets pop-up menu.

Note that the Motif palette includes different types of menus (pop-up, pull-down, option), but menus are *not* classes of widgets. Menus are discussed in Chapter 12.

When a widget is created on top of an existing widget that makes it a child of that existing widget, while one created on the desktop makes it a top-level widget. The parent of a widget may control the widget's size.

When beginning to build a new interface, a top-level widget must be created (i.e., a Shell widget, as discussed earlier) to be the parent of the other widgets. That Shell communicates with the window manager and acts as the parent for a single Manager widget, which in turn supports the rest of the interface.

Figure 11.1 shows how the top-level Shell is selected from the palette. The selection process is as follows.

1. Ensure that db-UIM/X is in Design mode.

2. Click with the mouse on the top-level Shell.

3. Move the mouse pointer (which has changed shape to a corner ⌐) to the point where the *upper-left corner* of the top-level widget is to be.

4. Press and hold the select mouse button, then drag the mouse down and to the *right* to draw the new widget (as would be the case when drawing a rectangle in a drawing program such as MacDraw or PowerPoint); the top-level Shell should be large enough to contain *two* pushbuttons.

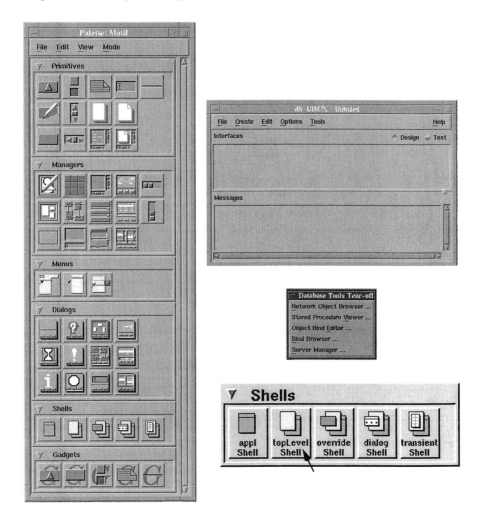

Figure 11.1 Selecting the top-level Shell from the Motif palette

At the point where the mouse button is released, the new widget is created by db-UIM/X (Figure 11.2) and is named `topLevelShell`.

Each top-level window in an application is called an *interface window* and is represented in the Interfaces Area of the Project Window as an icon (Figure 11.3).

The top-level Shell is automatically given eight *handles* through which resizing may be accomplished; at the point of creation, the widget is automatically selected (and the handles are shown). Resizing is accomplished in much the same way as in any desktop drawing program.

Figure 11.2 The top-level Shell after being created by the developer

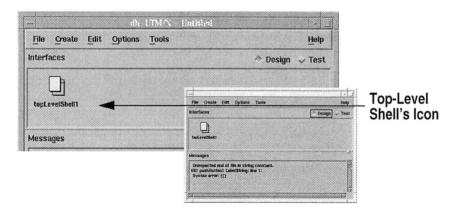

Top-Level
Shell's Icon

Figure 11.3 The top-level Shell's icon

CREATING THE MANAGER WIDGET

Typically, the first widget placed on a top-level Shell is a Manager widget, which in turn becomes the parent of the other widgets in the interface. For example, the Manager widget might be a form widget, which would be created as follows.

1. Again going to the Motif palette (as illustrated earlier), the Managers category would be accessed, from which the form button would be clicked.

2. The mouse pointer changes shape to a corner, indicating that the form can be created.

3. The select mouse button is pressed and held as the mouse is dragged to the dimensions and placement of the form.

4. Once the mouse button has been released, the form has been created.

At this point, the form widget has no special visual characteristics, so there is no noticeable change in the interface. Since the form is not a top-level Shell, there is no icon in the Project Window (i.e., it is a child of the top-level Shell).

SUMMARY

This chapter has provided a brief overview of the different types of shells and widgets and the beginnings of an example of creating different types of widgets for an interface (the top-level and the Manager). In the next chapter, we'll go into greater detail and create additional widgets, building a sample interface using db-UIM/X.

12

Drawing Interfaces

INTRODUCTION

In the previous chapter, we looked at the beginnings of creating (drawing) interfaces using db-UIM/X. In this chapter, we'll explore this subject in greater detail, discussing how programs are built, how menus are added to the interface, and other topics in the application creation domain.

CREATING ADDITIONAL WIDGETS

In the previous chapter, we showed examples of adding a Shell and Manager to the interface. Below are examples in which two different pushbuttons—one to activate the form dialog and another to exit from the application—are added. As was discussed in the previous chapter, pushbutton widgets are called *primitives* and serve as the "working parts" of the interfaces.

Going to the primitives part of the Motif palette (Figure 12.1), the pushButton button is clicked.

Just as with the other widgets, the mouse pointer changes to a corner (⌈), and the pushbutton can be drawn/dragged to the desired placement and dimensions. Once the mouse button is released, the new widget will automatically be named pushButton1 (Figure 12.2).

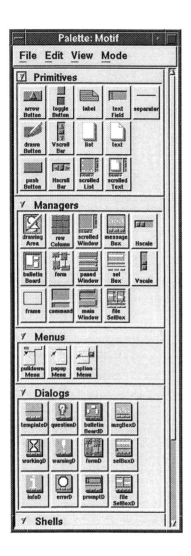

Figure 12.1 The Motif palette

By repeating the same steps as above, another pushbutton (pushButton2) can be created (Figure 12.3).

Every widget has nine invisible regions which are used for moving and resizing. The central region is used to move the widget, and any of the others are used to stretch or shrink the widget to a new size (just as the handles—as discussed in the previous chapter—are used to resize a win-

Figure 12.2 The new pushbutton

Figure 12.3 The interface with two pushbuttons

dow frame). If one widget is moved on top of another, the one that has been moved is automatically made a child of the other widget (assuming it is a valid parent). Once a parent-child relationship has been established, any new sizing and location information for a widget is reported to its parent, and it's possible that the parent will restrict or prohibit the attempted movement or resizing.

USING THE BROWSER

In Chapter 9, we introduced the Browser. Figure 12.4 shows how the Browser provides a graphical view of the widget hierarchy (a *widget tree*) from which widgets can be selected for operations.

When a box in the Browser (e.g., pushButton1) is selected, that widget will be selected as well in the interface window. The Browser can be used for complicated, large interfaces to locate a widget for operations such as resizing or movement.

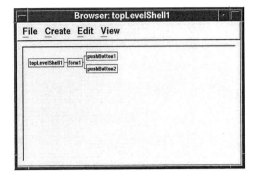

Figure 12.4 The widget Browser

EDITING LABELS

It is crucial to rename the widgets in the interface in accordance with the application being designed (e.g., something more meaningful than "pushButton1"). This is done by using the Widget Property Editor, which is invoked by double-clicking on a widget (e.g., pushButton1). The Prop-

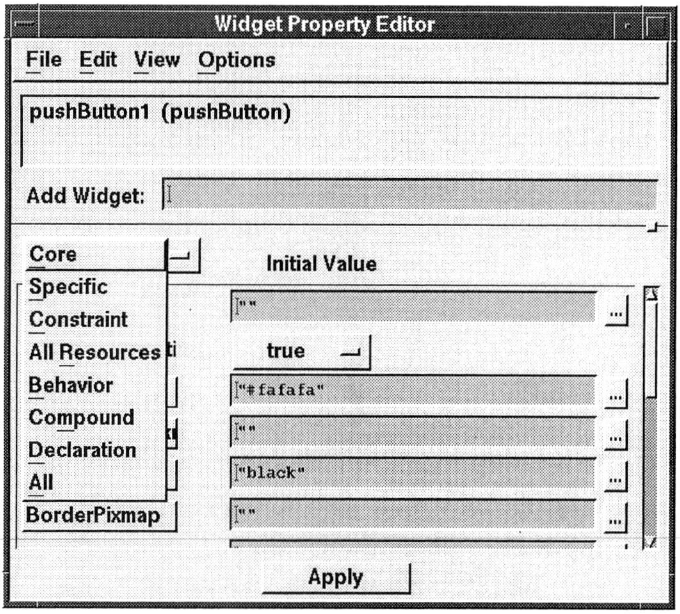

Figure 12.5 The property category option menu

Figure 12.6 The first button label changed

erty Editor presents the designer/developer with a number of properties
(Figure 12.5).

Properties are arranged into different categories, and the default category is "core" (i.e., the core properties of that particular widget). The
label Property Information is contained in the "Specific" category (selected from the menu), and LabelString contains the label name information (which, in actuality, is the widget resource XmNlabelString;
db-UIM/X handles the mappings behind the scenes). For example, Figure 12.6 shows how the pushbutton label name is changed to "Activate
Popup" by entering that string inside of quotation marks (" "). Figure 12.6
shows the interface with one of the pushbutton labels changed.

By leaving the Widget Property Editor menu open, the Options menu
can be used for a drag-and-drop change of the label of the second push-

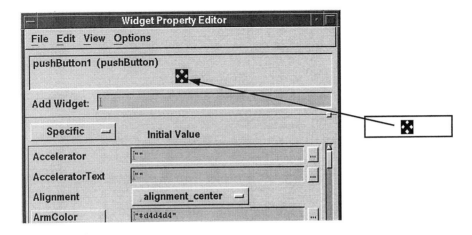

Figure 12.7 Using drag and drop with the Widget Property Editor

button (Figure 12.7). The Adjust mouse button is used, changing the pointer to a compass shape, and an outline of the pushbutton appears. The outline can be dragged to the Widget List area of the Widget Property Editor, the Specific properties will automatically be loaded, and "Exit" can be entered as the label.

CREATING A SECOND INTERFACE

The second interface—one designed to be popped up and down by pushbuttons—is a form dialog. This is created by clicking on the formDialog icon in the Dialogs category of the Motif palette and using the placement steps as with the other widgets. Note that the form dialog is both a Shell and a Manager (unlike with the first interface), so children can be created without having to explicitly create a separate Manager widget.

A text field widget (Figure 12.8) is then created, again following the selection and placement steps. It is often desirable to use *separators* to make visual divisions among the widgets; this primitive (Chapter 11) is chosen from the Motif palette and placed in the desired position beneath the text field widget. Figure 12.8 illustrates the text field, the separator, a label, and two pushbuttons with their label strings changed to "Text to Label" and "Close," respectively.

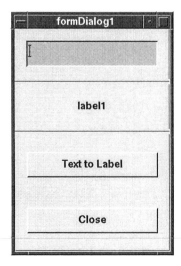

Figure 12.8 A second interface

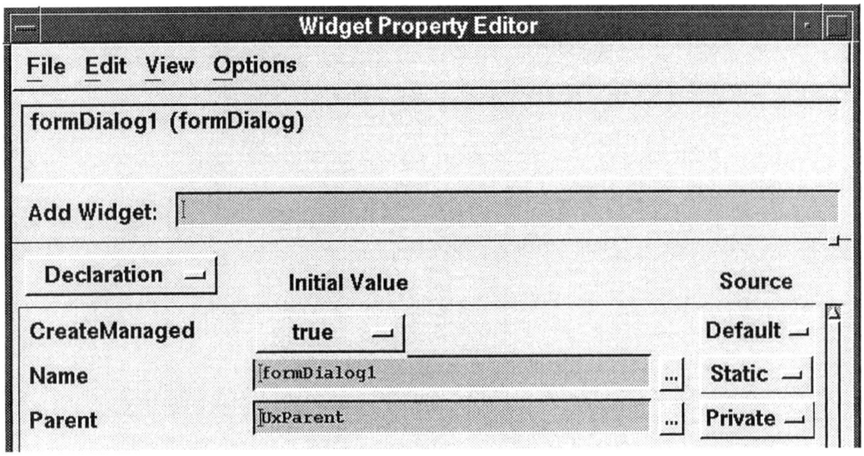

Figure 12.9 Showing the source column

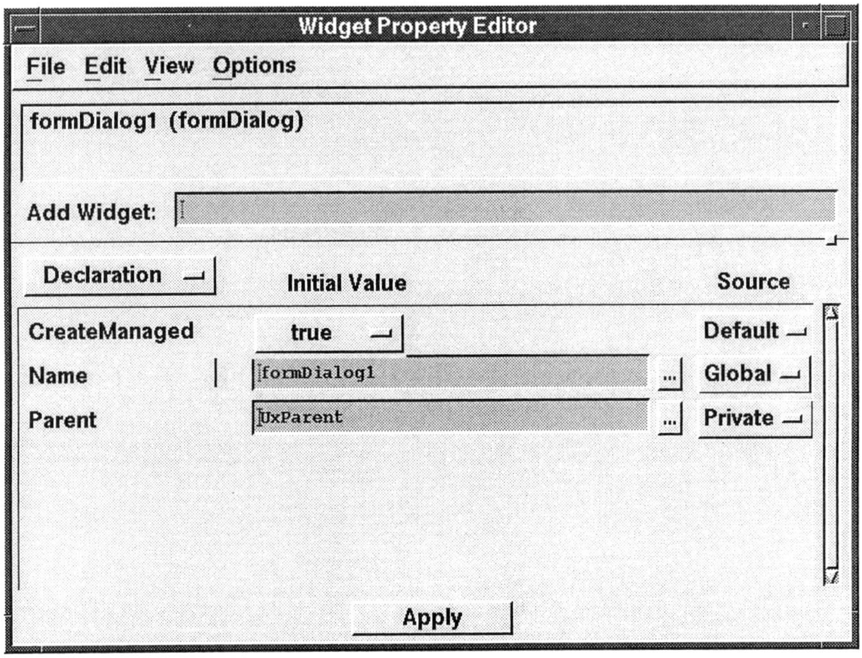

Figure 12.10 Changing the interface to global

When the developer writes the C code for these two interfaces, a source file will be created for each one. Because the Activate Popup pushbutton in the first interface references the second interface, that second interface must be made global. This is done by opening the Property Editor . . . accomplished by moving the mouse pointer to the center of formDialog1 and dragging and dropping the outline of formDialog1 into the Widget Property Editor to load its properties. In the Declaration category, the "Hide Source" option should be turned *off*, making the Source column for each property visible (Figure 12.9).

The source for formDialog1 should then be changed from "Static" to "Global" (Figure 12.10).

USING THE DECLARATIONS EDITOR

By clicking on any widget in the topLevelShell1 interface window, the Declarations Editor may be accessed, in which a text editor is available for the C declarations code that must be included. Figure 12.11 shows the extern and swidget statements that should be added.

The Declarations Editor then contains the added statements (Figure 12.12).

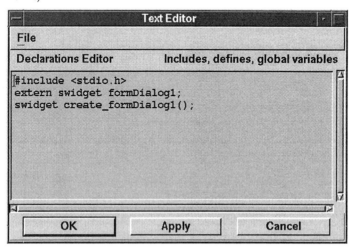

Figure 12.11 The Text Editor used for declarations

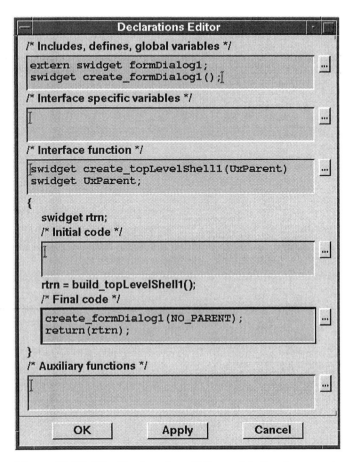

Declarations Editor

```
/* Includes, defines, global variables */

extern swidget formDialog1;
swidget create_formDialog1();

/* Interface specific variables */



/* Interface function */

swidget create_topLevelShell1(UxParent)
swidget UxParent;

{
    swidget rtrn;
    /* Initial code */



    rtrn = build_topLevelShell1();
    /* Final code */

    create_formDialog1(NO_PARENT);
    return(rtrn);

}
/* Auxiliary functions */



    OK          Apply          Cancel
```

Figure 12.12 The Declarations Editor with developer-entered changes

ADDING BEHAVIOR

So far, the examples have focused on the visual aspects of the interface. In this section, we'll discuss how behavior is added to the interfaces.

PushButton1—now labeled "Activate Popup"—should be double-clicked, again loading it into the Property Editor. The "Behavior" option (refer to Figure 12.5) is selected, and several different text fields are presented.

- ActivateCallback
- ActivateClientData

- ArmCallback

- ArmClientData

In the ActivateCallback field, the following C code should be entered:

```
UxPopupInterface (formDialog1, no_grab) ;
```

Doing the same for pushButton2 (now labeled "Exit"), the ActivateCall-back field should be entered as:

```
Exit (0) ;
```

In the second interface, the desired effect is that whenever the user clicks on the Text To Label pushbutton, any text that had been entered into the text field is copied into the label. If the form's dialog resources aren't changed, though, the form will be popped down (i.e., hidden) whenever the Text To Label pushbutton is clicked. This is because the form dialog inherits a bulletin board resource called XmNautoUnmanage—the default value of which is "True"—meaning that if the parent is a dialog Shell the form dialog is unmanaged whenever a pushbutton is pressed. This resource must be set to "False," again using the Widget Property Editor (Figure 12.13).

Behavior for the pushbuttons in formDialog1 is then set, according to the following steps.

1. The Text To Label pushbutton is dragged into the Widget Property Editor.

2. "Behavior" is chosen (if it isn't already showing).

3. The following C code is entered into ActivateCallback:

```
UxPutLabelString (label1, UxGetText (textField1));
```

(The two "Ux" functions in the code are part of the Ux Convenience Library.)

To establish the behavior of the Close pushbutton—popping down the interface window—a db-UIM/X library function is used.

1. The Close pushbutton is dragged and dropped into the Property Editor.

2. In the ActivateCallback field, the library function is entered:

```
UxPopdownInterface (formDialog1);
```

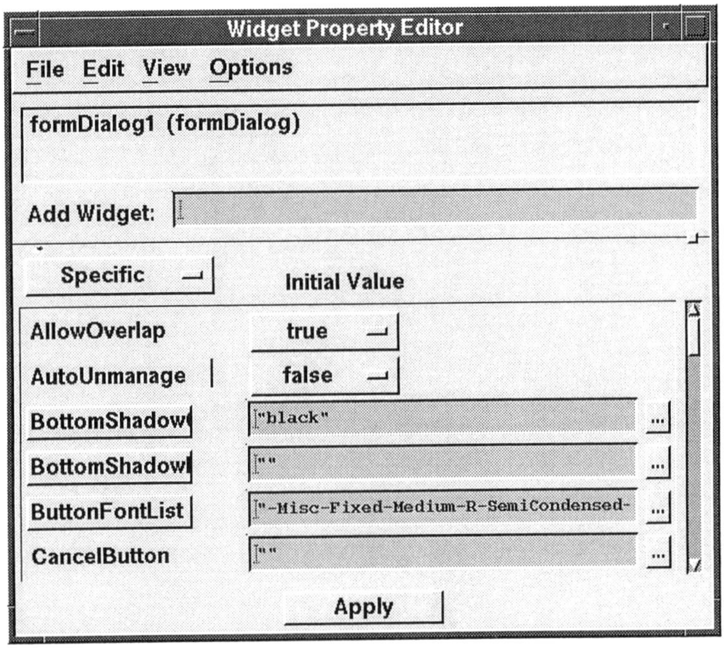

Figure 12.13 The formDialog1 Widget Property Editor

TESTING THE INTERFACES

As was discussed in earlier chapters, the interfaces can be tested from within the db-UIM/X environment. The Test toggle button in the Project Window is clicked, and the developer can use the mouse actions desired (e.g., clicking the Close pushbutton) to verify that all of the widgets have been designed properly and have had appropriate behavior assigned to them.

WRITING C CODE

At this point, the C code can be generated. db-UIM/X must be in Design mode. Following selection of Code Generation from the Options menu, the developer is given several different code generation options (Figure 12.14).

After the options have been selected, the Generate Project Code As... menu choice will bring up the dialog shown in Figure 12.15.

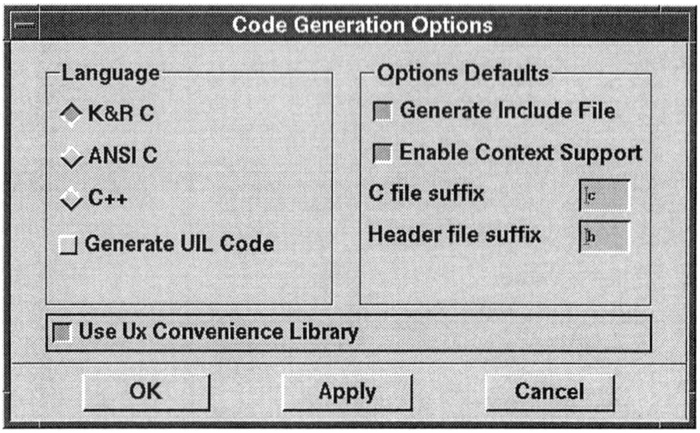

Figure 12.14 The Code Generation Options dialog

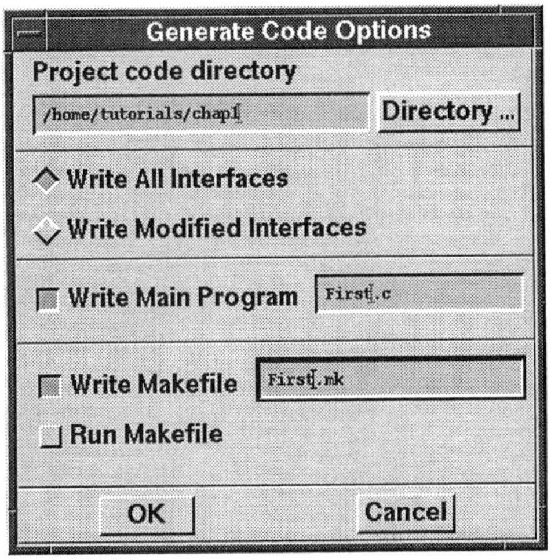

Figure 12.15 The Generate Code Options dialog

db-UIM/X will generate code for all of the interfaces, plus the makefile. If "Run Makefile" is selected, the program will be compiled automatically.

BUILDING A WORKING APPLICATION WITH DB-UIM/X

In this section, we'll expand our discussion of db-UIM/X to demonstrate how to build a simple working application, including menus for that

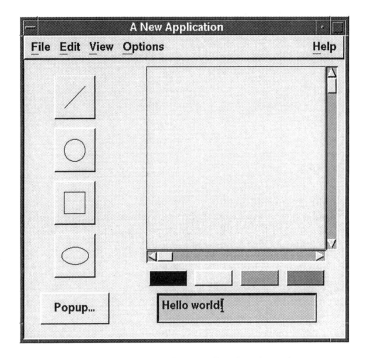

Figure 12.16 A simple drawing application interface

application. Figure 12.16 shows the application—a simple drawing program—that will be built.

For the sake of this book, much of the "overhead" (e.g., setting the db-UIM/X environment, descriptions of mouse movements, etc.) will not be included; complete, step-by-step details can be found in db-UIM/X documentation material.

As has been discussed earlier, the first step is to ensure that db-UIM/X is in Design mode (rather than Test mode). Within the Motif palette, the "Frame" button on the Manager palette is selected, and the developer then draws the frame widget on the interface (Figure 12.17).

The next step is to make the frame scrollable, which is done by selecting vertScrollBar and horizScrollBar from the Primitives area of the Motif palette (one after the other, drawing the respective scroll bars on the desired places on the frame). Figure 12.18 shows the frame after the scroll bars have been drawn.

(Note: When building a production application, the scrolled window widget [Chapter 11] could be used as a step saver instead of each individual widget.)

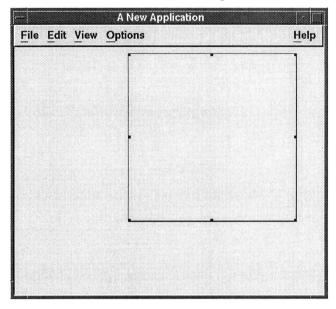

Figure 12.17 The frame widget

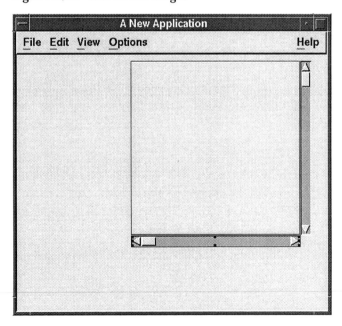

Figure 12.18 The frame after the scroll bars have been drawn

The scroll bars could then be moved and resized as necessary to get the desired placement.

The next step is to add a pushbutton—which will be used to change the color of the drawing area—in the same manner as pushbuttons were added in the example earlier in this chapter. The properties (color, widget name, etc.) would then be changed (again, by dragging the pushbutton into the Widget Property Editor).

Note that there is a lot of activity going on while using db-UIM/X in Design mode. A suggested manner of managing the real estate of one's screen (e.g., how the windows are arranged) is shown in Figure 12.19. Note that the application for which the interface is being designed is in the upper right-hand side of the screen, the db-UIM/X controls are in the upper left, and the Widget Property Editor is in the bottom left-hand side.

With respect to setting the properties for the pushbutton, a Color Viewer is brought up from which a color may be selected for the background of the pushbutton (Figure 12.20).

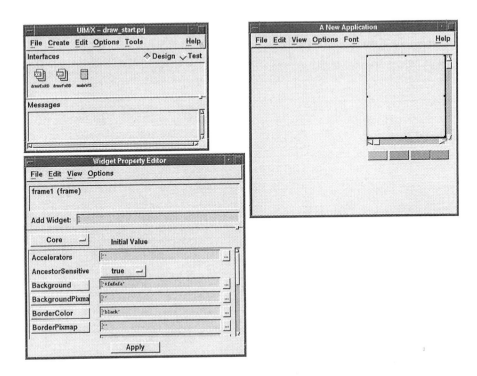

Figure 12.19 Recommended arrangement of db-UIM/X screen

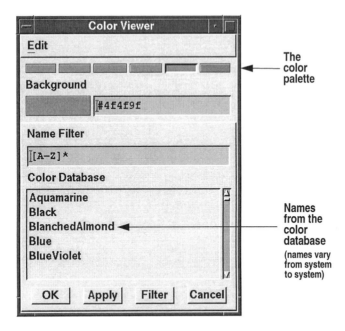

Figure 12.20 The Color Viewer

(If desired, the color may be edited using the Color Editor; the hue, saturation, and intensity of the color may be adjusted and custom colors created.)

Another property that can be changed is the font (in this case, that of the pushbutton's label). Figure 12.21 shows the Font Viewer and the selections that can be made.

The next step is to create three additional pushbuttons (for this application), arrange them in the desired places on the interface, and change the background colors of each in the same manner as described above. Figure 12.22 shows the state of the interface after these steps have been accomplished.

One of the things that hasn't been discussed yet with respect to db-UIM/X is the use of menus in the interface. The next steps discuss how a pull-down menu is added.

The first step is to select Options on the interface's menu bar, and, from that menu, the Menu Editor. As shown in Figure 12.23, the MenuBar Editor appears.

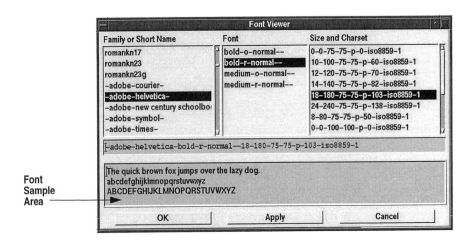

Font
Sample
Area

Figure 12.21 The Font Viewer

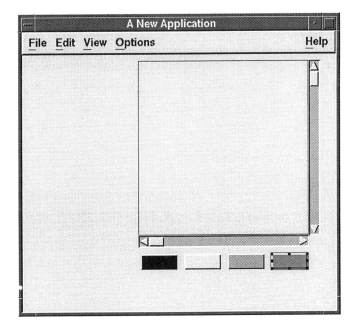

Figure 12.22 The interface after the pushbuttons have been put in place

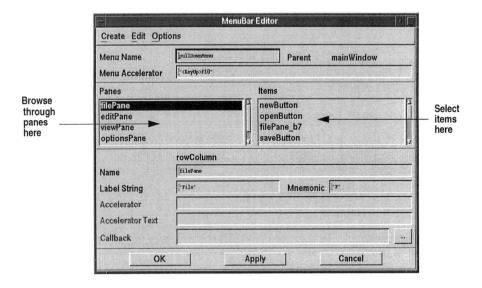

Figure 12.23 The MenuBar Editor in db-UIM/X

In this application, a menu from which multiple fonts are selected is part of the interface. This is added to the interface by doing the following.

1. Create is selected from the MenuBar Editor, and then Pane is chosen (to create a pane).

2. In the Name field, the name `fontPane` is entered.

3. In the Label String field, `Font` is entered (this is the name that will appear on the menu bar).

4. In the Mnemonic field, "n" is entered (between double quotes).

5. Create and Item After are the next selections, and pushButton is chosen; `courButton` is added as the Name, `Courier` is entered as the Label String, and "c" as the Mnemonic.

6. The other font choices (e.g., Helvetica, etc.) are added as choices.

The Browser can be used to browse the widget hierarchy after the rest of the buttons and menu choices have been created (Figure 12.24).

As was described earlier in this chapter, callback behavior is added to each of the widgets, and the desired callback behavior is added using the

Double-click on a widget icon
to show or hide its children

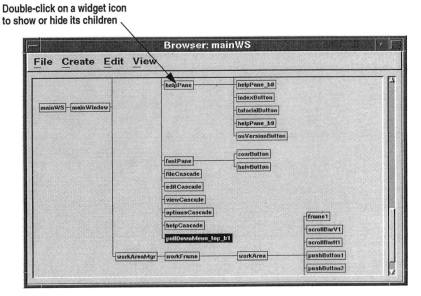

Figure 12.24 The widget Browser (again)

appropriate library functions. In this particular application, though, drawing behavior is also needed. This is done in the following manner.

The first step is to compose event strings, which is done by selecting a widget on the interface and popping up the Selected Widgets menu. Other/Translations is chosen, bringing up the Translation Table List for the project. The Translation Table Editor is then brought up (Figure

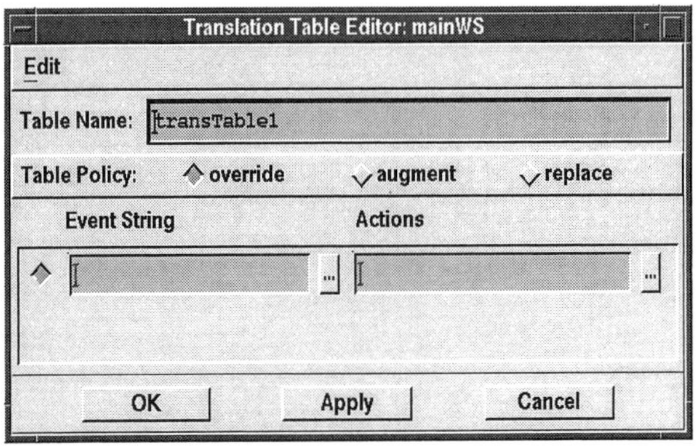

Figure 12.25 The Translation Table Editor

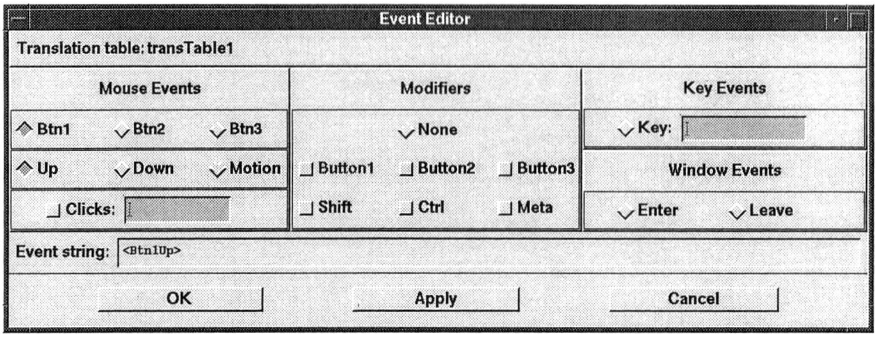

Figure 12.26 The Event Editor

12.25), in which event strings (e.g., button presses) are paired with the appropriate C code actions to be executed when the event occurs. Any X Toolkit event may be entered in the event string. An Event Editor is provided to help you compose event strings for common events.

In this particular application, three event strings need to be composed. For the first event string, the Mouse Events area is entered and the Btn1 and Down radio buttons are pressed; this results in the event string of <Btn1Down>. The next one, done in the same way, results in <Btn1Motion>, and the last one results in <Btn1Up> (the last one is shown in Figure 12.26).

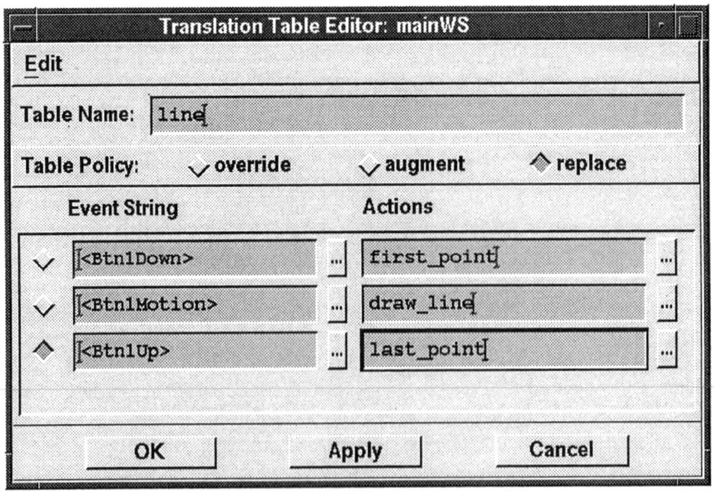

Figure 12.27 The Translation Table and event strings for drawing lines

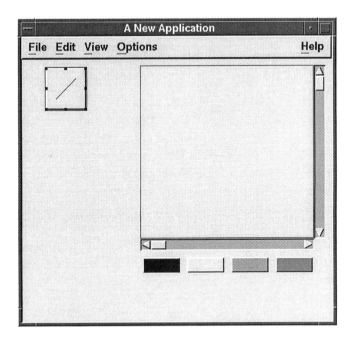

Figure 12.28 The first line drawing pushbutton with its pixmap

After defining the events, the next step is to specify the actions to be added to the Translation Table—those that will enable the application's user to draw a line. Figure 12.27 shows the Translation Table for the events; the table name is changed to "line" and the Translation Table is completed.

As is common in drawing programs, pushbutton controls, through which the user specifies the type of object he or she wishes to draw, can be used. The pushbutton examples described earlier in this chapter all use text labels; alternatively, pixmap files containing graphical images can be used. By using the Pixmap viewer, the interface can evolve to the point shown in Figure 12.28.

THE REST OF THE APPLICATION

The rest of the application creation process proceeds using a combination of the db-UIM/X tools and editors described in this chapter (e.g., the Callback Editor, the Declarations Editor, the Pixmap Viewer, etc.). Interested readers are directed to the db-UIM/X documentation for the step-by-step details.

MAKING REUSABLE INTERFACES

Once interfaces have been created, it's often desirable to reuse elements in several places. However, as is the case with code in general, simple duplication means that subsequent changes would have to be repeated in many places.

A better approach is to build a Component as a separate interface and create an Instance of the Component in the other interfaces, as is common in object-oriented systems. Using O-O terminology, a Component would be a class, and an Instance is an object of that class. It is also possible to create Subclasses of a Component, thereby creating a class hierarchy using inheritance and method overloading.

In db-UIM/X a Component is a top-level interface. Instances of Components can be created that are present either as interfaces in the project or as generated C code. In the latter case, the C code can be either compiled and linked to db-UIM/X or loaded into the C Interpreter.

For example, an instance of a BulletinBoard interface containing a Label and a TextField widget is used in another interface, and the Instance looks and behaves as defined in the Component. Changes made to the Component are *immediately* reflected in all its instances.

Like classes in O-O languages, Components have a constructor, properties, and methods. The constructor is the function that builds Instances.

By default, an Instance has no editable properties . . . it inherits its properties from the Component. Properties that *are* editable in the Instance are made available by adding arguments to the Interface Function of the Component. Any editable property of an Instance appears in the Property Editor in the Specific category.

Methods can be defined for Components, as they can for any interface, and an Instance of any Component can be saved in the palette for future use and can be shared among other users.

Some other items of note follow.

- A Subclass of a Component is a top-level Instance of that Component. Like all top-level interfaces, a Subclass has its own constructor and properties.

- Creating Instances of Components produces considerably less code than mere duplication. Instances work by calling the Interface Function of the Component they reference.

- Initial and final code written in the Declarations of a Component is executed when the Component's constructor is called. db-UIM/X calls the constructor when you create, move, resize, or change the properties of an Instance of the Component. In general, the constructor is called every time you cause the Instance to be recreated.

- By designating one widget from the Component as a child site, any Instance of the Component can be made to accept children.

Creating a Component

Any top-level interface (discussed in earlier chapters) is a potential Component. The following rules govern the use of interfaces as Components.

- A Component must take a swidget as the first argument of its Interface Function.

- The first argument to the Interface Function must be used as the Parent specified in the Declaration category of the Property Editor.

- The CreateManaged property of the Component should be set to "false." If set to "true," the placement of the Instance in its parent can become unpredictable. (Interfaces other than Components generally need this property set to "true," so db-UIM/X automatically sets this property to "true" when an interface is created.)

Setting the Component's CreateManaged property to "false" ensures that instances of the Component are placed properly. However, if the Component itself is used as the startup interface or as a top-level interface, the UxManage() Convenience Library Function must be called; this function manages an interface that has its CreateManaged property set to "false." Example:

```
swidget f1;
f1 = create_form1 (NO_PARENT) ;
UxManage (f1);
```

Promoting a Widget to Top-Level

If the widget that is to serve as a Component already resides in an interface (i.e., it was created before the reusability was desired), it must first be made a top-level interface. Any widget except a gadget or menu can be promoted to a top-level interface. This is done by simply dragging the widget onto the desktop. A dialog will ask the developer if he or she wants to replace the original widget with an Instance of the Component (which should be answered in the affirmative).

Adding Editable Properties to an Instance

Editable properties can be added to an Instance by adding arguments to a Component's Interface Function (constructor). These arguments are listed as the Specific properties of the Instance in the Property Editor.

Instance property values are matched to Component arguments by name; so if an argument name is changed, the values entered under the previous name are discarded.

Creating an Instance

The means by which instances can be created as children of other widgets are as follows.

1. First, an Instance must never be placed in a widget hierarchy where one of its ancestors is the Component; the circular nesting can send the Interpreter into an infinite loop.

2. An Instance, like any other widget, cannot be placed in a widget that does not accept children. For example, pushbutton widgets do not accept children.

3. The Component is selected.

4. The Selected Widget's pop-up menu (for the parent manager) is accessed, and Instance is chosen from the interfaceName selections.

5. At the point where the left corner shape is set for the pointer, db-UIM/X will modify the Instance menu selection to offer the selected interface as a potential Component.

6. The pointer is dragged over the parent to create the Instance, creating (in this case) interfaceNameInstance1.

Creating a Subclass

A Subclass is a stand-alone interface, which inherits all content and methods of its base Component. Subclasses are used to build a class hierarchy where each Subclass can add its own children, properties, and methods, as well as inherit or override the methods it inherits from its base class.

Using the Project Window Create menu, Subclass of interfaceName is selected and the developer drags the pointer over empty space on the desktop to create the Subclass (named interfaceNameSubclass1).

SUMMARY

This chapter has covered the basics of creating interfaces—including reusable ones—within db-UIM/X. db-UIM/X does contain additional details and examples. For our purposes, though, we've investigated the basics of creating an interface using the db-UIM/X facilities. In the next chapter, we'll shift our discussion of db-UIM/X facilities to look at the Network Object Toolkit, as our discussion shifts into the client/server application architecture realm.

13

The Network Object Toolkit

INTRODUCTION

As discussed previously, open client/server computing gives architects and designers a vast array of options with respect to the partitioning and construction of applications and systems. As visual development tools first came to prominence, there was a tendency for product offerings in the marketplace to be "client-centric," that is, they concentrated on client-side functionality at the expense of the server (or, more recently) middleware components. In effect, multiple development environments were typically needed for the client and server sides.

A product such as db-UIM/X, however, provides a development environment that covers both the client and server sides of the application. In the previous chapters, we've looked at how the client sides of applications are constructed using db-UIM/X widgets to form interfaces. In this chapter, we'll begin to shift our discussion to the server side of the application architecture, discussing the Network Object Toolkit.

The Network Object Toolkit is a suite of components through which the developer can link GUI application components created with db-UIM/X (e.g., of the types created in the examples in the previous chapters) with objects of relational database management system (RDBMS) engines. These tools include:

- Network Object Browser
- Network Object Editor
- Object Results Viewer
- Object Bind Editor
- Network Object Selector
- Bind Browser
- Database Login Dialog
- Server/Database Manager
- Bind Manager

Some of the individual components contain a Tools Menu, which allows access to the major Network Object Toolkit components. Additionally, the Project Window's Database pull-down menu can be used for such access.

The purpose of the Network Object Toolkit is to bind object input and output to other objects, yielding a final results set known as an *object binding*. The *Map* is a dynamic list of all of these object bindings and is created and maintained within the Network Object Toolkit.

NETWORK OBJECT TYPES

Currently, db-UIM/X supports two Object Types:

- stored procedures
- DSQL objects

These objects reside on the network and can be bound to the GUI components, creating a client/server application.

Stored Procedures

Stored procedures are SQL objects that are stored in a database and maintained by the database itself. They accept arguments that are used as variables throughout the SQL contained in the stored procedures. In effect, they are one of the primary mechanisms through which application logic is pushed into the database server in a client/server environment.

Stored procedures can be created using the tools that come with DBMSs having that capability (nearly every RDBMS product does), or they can be created from within db-UIM/X by using the Network Object Editor. As most readers are aware, each vendor has its own distinct stored procedure implementation (although with the SQL3 standard it is expected that over time, as a standardized stored procedure language is accepted and approved, the languages from the various vendors will converge . . . but it is not likely they will ever be identical—no more so than their SQL commands are).

DSQL Objects

Dynamic SQL permits the user to bind GUI objects to vendor-specific SQL objects called DSQL. DSQL objects are defined by the database vendor being used in an environment (e.g., those of Sybase and ORACLE are different from one another), just as stored procedure languages differ from product to product.

DSQL objects are saved in an environment's mass storage (i.e., on disk) using a certain naming convention that again varies from product to product. db-UIM/X needs to know where to read and write DSQL objects at start-up, and, if the environment variable DSQLDIR is set to point to a directory path, db-UIM/X will look in that path. Otherwise, if no DSQLDIR environment variable is set, db-UIM/X looks in the project's directory.

Binding DSQL objects is equivalent to binding stored procedures, except that there is no return status.[*] The bindings consist of Activators, Arguments (placeholders), and results data.

CREATING DSQL OBJECTS

The Network Object Editor is used to create a DSQL object (and also to create and modify stored procedures). The Network Object Editor usage is described later in this chapter.

---

[*] Note that currently there is no return status for ORACLE stored procedures, although this may change with future versions of the ORACLE engine.

DSQL uses placeholders to facilitate user input, WHERE CLAUSE support, and dynamic SQL capabilities. When creating DSQL objects, the SQL statement(s) is typed in with room left for placeholders. Placeholders are marked using a pound sign (#) to denote the beginning and ending with information for IDs, the native vendor's data type, and default values (the latter for Sybase only). Examples will be shown later in this chapter.

THE NETWORK OBJECT BROWSER

The Network Object Browser interface allows the user to view the data dictionary for the chosen database server. Its primary function is to provide a reference when binding database objects to Graphical User Interface objects. The interface allows the user to configure its size and contents dynamically by utilizing the View menu and the pop-up menus associated with each list. Figure 13.1 shows the Network Object Browser.

The following information is displayed in the Network Object Browser, as illustrated in Figure 13.1.

- Servers

- Databases

- Tables/Views

- Columns

- Objects

- Object Arguments

Servers, Databases, Tables, Views, and Columns

The Servers list provides a list of all the RDBMS servers recognized by the Object Request Broker (ORB). These servers are obtained from the ORB each time a Network Object Browser is invoked, ensuring that a "fresh" list is available (particularly desirable in a dynamic environment). For example, the server named ORACLE will provide a list of ORACLE databases.

The database list will depend on the specifics of the database server product. Currently, with Sybase, the system catalog for the selected server is scanned for all of the databases it contains when a server is selected as

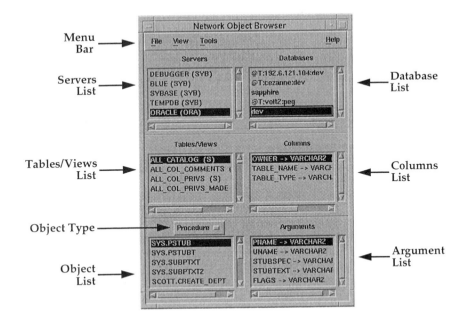

Figure 13.1 The Network Object Browser

described above. With ORACLE, the db-ORB is queried for all of the ORACLE Database connection strings with which it is familiar.

Once a database has been selected, the system catalog for the selected database is scanned for all of the tables belonging to the selected database. The tables are grouped by type (slight differences exist between Sybase and ORACLE databases . . . Sybase presents system tables while ORACLE presents user synonyms; otherwise, though, both present user tables and views) and presented to the user in a Tables/Views List.

Drilling even further, the selection of a table causes the system catalog to be scanned for all columns belonging to that table. The columns and associated data are displayed in the Columns List in the order in which they were created. Information about column name, data type, dimension, and null status is presented.

The Object List and Arguments

When a database is selected, the objects associated with the database are displayed in the Object List. Depending on the selection of the object type option menu, the developer will be presented with stored procedures or DSQL objects.

When an object is selected, the system catalog is scanned for all of the arguments belonging to the selected object.

THE NETWORK OBJECT SELECTOR

The Network Object Selector is used to load objects into the Object Bind Editor and the Network Object Editor, and it operates somewhat differently depending on which mode it is in (Procedure mode or DSQL mode). Figure 13.2 shows the Network Object Selector in procedure mode.

THE NETWORK OBJECT EDITOR

The Network Object Editor is used to create new DSQL objects and stored procedures and to modify those already existing. It also allows the granting/revoking of execute privileges, deleting objects, and testing results sets that an object is capable of returning. The viewing of test data takes

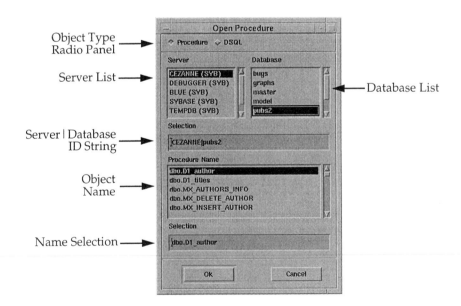

Figure 13.2 The Network Object Selector in procedure mode

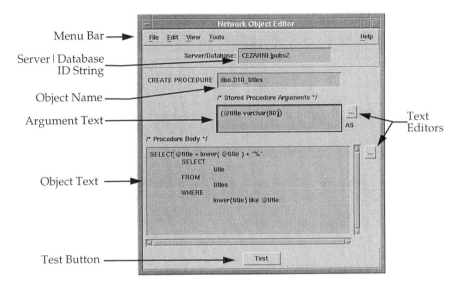

Figure 13.3 The Network Object Editor in procedure mode

place in the Object Results Viewer, discussed later in the chapter. Figure 13.3 shows the Network Object Editor for stored procedures, and Figure 13.4 shows the Network Object Editor for DSQL mode.

Privileges are granted or revoked on stored procedures by first opening the object that is to be changed. Once the object has been loaded into the Network Object Editor, the Privileges Dialog (Figure 13.5) can be selected

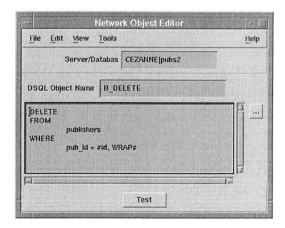

Figure 13.4 The Network Object Editor in DSQL mode

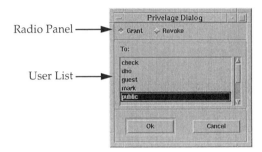

Radio Panel ⟶

User List ⟶

Figure 13.5 The Privileges Dialog

in which the granting or revoking of a procedure to various users (or public) can be accomplished.

THE OBJECT RESULTS VIEWER

The Object Results Viewer allows the developer to view one set of results from an object loaded into the Network Object Editor, as discussed earlier. Figure 13.6 shows an Object Results Viewer example.

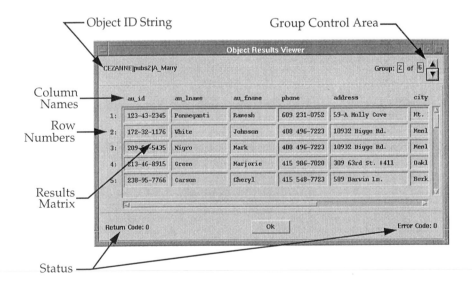

Figure 13.6 The Object Results Viewer

By using different argument values in the Argument Dialog a variety of results sets can be obtained, enabling the database server side of an application to be tested.

THE OBJECT BIND EDITOR

So far, the components of the Network Object Toolkit seem to stand alone, that is, they appear to be a set of tools that work with the database side of an application but have little interoperability among themselves and with the client side. The Object Bind Editor—the most complex interface of the Network Object Toolkit—is where the binding relationships among objects are made; in effect, it functions as the glue for much of the environment.

The Object Bind Editor is used to bind:

- stored procedures
- DSQL objects
- cached data resulting from an object's execution
- GUI components

Figure 13.7 shows the Object Bind Editor.

Each of the areas and controls shown in Figure 13.7 is discussed in this section.

The Object Bindings List is the area that keeps track of the object bindings a developer has in the Map for the current project. Figure 13.8 shows a sample Object Bindings List.

Each item in the list contains:

- the object type (either stored procedure or DSQL)
- the database vendor (currently either ORACLE or Sybase)
- the binding relationship (one of three values):

    —NONE—the cache is not being used—meaning object results are being bound to widgets or that the object has no results

    —TO—bind an object's results to a local memory cache and/or to selected GUI components

    —FROM—take data from the memory cache instead of executing the object again

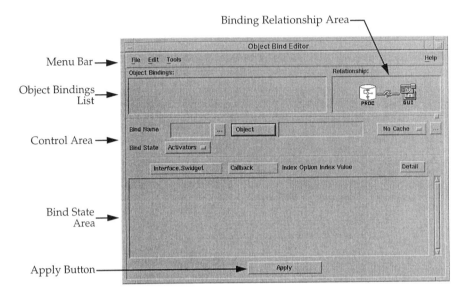

Figure 13.7 The Object Bind Editor

- a bind name, which is a unique way of identifying an object binding
- an object ID string (used within db-UIM/X)

The Binding Relationship Area is used as a quick visual reference to the type of binding currently loaded into the Object Bind Editor. Figure 13.9 shows a stored procedure bound to a GUI object, and the set of pixmaps is shown in Figure 13.10.

The control area has several purposes, including:

- displaying global data about the current binding
- loading objects and object bindings into the Object Bind Editor

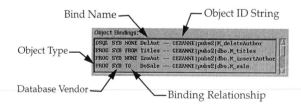

Figure 13.8 The Object Bindings List

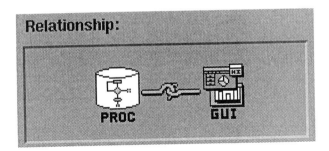

Figure 13.9 A GUI object-to-stored procedure binding

Figure 13.10 The pixmaps used for binding relationships

- configuring the cache options
- changing the current bind state

Figure 13.11 shows an example of the Control Area.

The Bind State Area is where all of the individual object component bindings are made. There are three distinct bind states for each binding.

1. Activators: These are the events or actions that need to take place in order for an object to be executed. In most cases activators will be a widget's callback. An object binding must have at least one activator and can have as many as necessary.

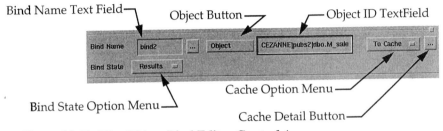

Figure 13.11 The Object Bind Editor Control Area

2. Arguments: Each object binding can have a list of arguments passed to it at execution time. These data qualify how an object will be executed and what results will be returned. Data can be hard-coded or provided from other objects. Caches do not have arguments, and arguments are not mandatory.

3. Results: Results are all of the data resulting from an object binding's execution. Results data are returned in a Result Group/Row/Column format and also include any status/error messages returned by the process of execution.

In db-UIM/X all of the object binding states are performed through a graphical means in the three separate states of the Object Bind Editor. The first state is the Activator Bind State (the default when a new object is loaded), in which the activator behavior is configured and the object execution is specified. Figure 13.12 shows the Activator Bind State.

When the Swidget Selector comes up, the Interface list contains all of the interfaces that have been created in the current project (see Chapter 12 for a discussion of creating interfaces). When an interface is selected from the list, all of its swidgets will appear in the Swidget list. The combination is assembled into an Interface/Swidget ID string in the Selection Text Field.

The Callback Selector is a means of choosing a callback for a given swidget class. When the Selector is invoked, it determines the class of the swidget INITs associated with the Interface/Swidget Text Field. The Se-

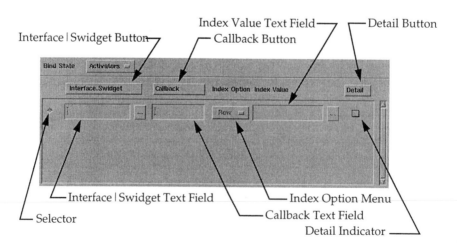

Figure 13.12 The Activator Bind State

lector then populates its scrolled list with all of the valid callback names for that swidget class. If the Interface/Swidget Text Field does not contain a valid Interface/Swidget ID, the Callback Selector will not pop up.

The Activator Detail Editor allows the developer to fine-tune the way in which an object binding is activated. Figure 13.13 shows that editor.

With respect to Figure 13.13, the Mode is an option menu that permits the developer to specify one of three modes in which the object can be executed.

1. *Synchronous* (the default),which means that the object binding will wait for all of the results to be returned before the next instruction is carried out in the application code.

2. *Asynchronous cancel,* which means that the application will not wait for the results to come back before the next instruction is carried out. A dialog will be presented to the user to permit cancellation of the execution if so desired.

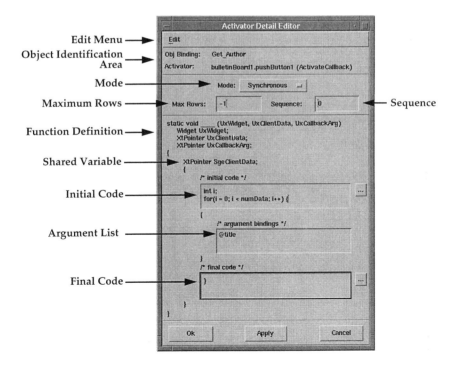

Figure 13.13 The Activator Detail Editor

3. *Asynchronous no cancel,* which is the same as above but does not permit user-driven cancellation.

Other details that can be specified include the maximum number of rows the database will return for a given object binding's execution (used as a safety valve and for debugging) and the areas in which code to be executed can be specified.

The other facilities of the Object Bind Editor are discussed in the db-UIM/X product documentation.

THE BIND BROWSER

Once object bindings have been produced with the Object Bind Editor, it is often convenient to see the binding relationships all in one place. The Bind Browser (Figure 13.14) supports this.

The Bind Browser allows the developer to view the binding relationships in two ways. The first method is by selecting an object binding and seeing all of the swidgets bound to its results column with all of the

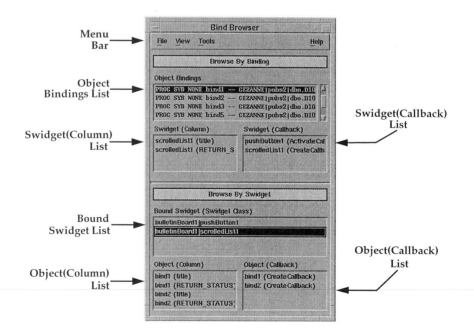

Figure 13.14 The Bind Browser

activators for the selected object binding. This takes place in the upper half of the Bind Browser (Figure 13.14). The second method is by selecting the Interface/Swidget combination and seeing all of the object binding results columns to which it is bound and/or all of the object bindings for which it is an activator. This takes place in the lower half of the Bind Browser.

THE DATABASE LOGIN DIALOG

The Database Login Dialog is used to get login information when a valid login has not already been specified. It automatically prompts the user when a login is necessary.

The first time a login is specified for any server or database, it automatically becomes the Default Server/Database. That is because the first login is the first entry in the Login List. If a first Login List item exists, its information is tried first on all requests whose server/database has no login information. If the default login fails for a server/database that has no login information explicitly set, the Database Login Dialog will pop up and prompt the user for a correct login.

Aliases may be specified so that when a server/database is called by the application, the server/database alias will be called instead. For example, if an object binding is set up to run on server A, but the user wishes to run the object binding on server B, the user would specify server B as the alias. Until the alias is reset to NULL, all procedures executed for server A will actually attempt to execute on server B. A common use of this is taking an application from testing against a development database server into production against the live database. In mix-and-match client/server environments with multiple servers, this is a valuable facility because it alleviates a lot of 3GL-based or command language–based redirection.

In client applications, the Database Login Dialog allows aliases to be indicated by overwriting the server/database name with the server/database name to use as the alias. Once the alias is specified, the Username and Password must be entered for the alias server, and "OK" should be clicked.

THE SERVER/DATABASE MANAGER

The Server/Database Manager is used to manage server information for db-UIM/X. It has two modes (depending on which DBMS vendor is selected, Sybase or ORACLE). Figure 13.15 shows the Sybase mode.

A list of Sybase servers (or ORACLE databases) and their login information is maintained automatically by the tool and all of the clients generated by the tool. The first login is the default login and can be provided in three ways:

1. the login screen
2. the API function call *SaAddLoginRec()*
3. the Server/Database Manager (only in db-UIM/X, not in clients)

The default login is tried first for all requests whose server or database has no login information. All subsequent logins are added to the list and used when requests are made from a server or database. Aliases may be specified so that whenever a server or database is called by the application, the alias will be used instead.

The Server/Database Manager has several purposes.

1. It specifies logins for database servers on the network that are known to the Object Request Broker.
2. It chooses which login information is used as the default login. The default login is tried first for each request whose server or database

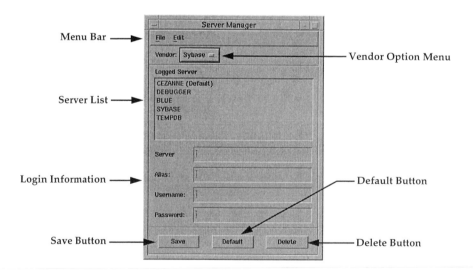

Figure 13.15 The Server Manager (Sybase mode)

has no login information; however, if that default login fails, the user is prompted for the information.

3. It changes login information for a selected server or database.

4. It removes logins for selected servers or databases (useful when testing clients).

5. It specifies a server alias (as discussed earlier).

THE BIND MANAGER

The final component of the Network Object Toolkit is the Bind Manager, which allows a developer to make binding substitutions globally or selectively. Using the Bind Manager, the developer may change:

- Vendors
- Servers
- Databases
- Owners
- Objects

Figure 13.16 shows the Server Mapper dialog of the Bind Manager.

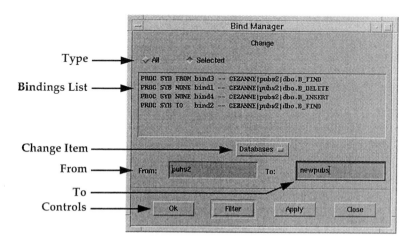

Figure 13.16 The Server Mapper dialog

SUMMARY

In this chapter, we've looked at the various components of the Network Object Toolkit—those used to manage the database server side of applications within the db-UIM/X environment. As in the previous chapter, we have only presented a brief overview, and the reader is directed to the appropriate db-UIM/X documentation for more detailed discussions and examples.

In the next chapter, we'll examine how to integrate cross-platform components.

14

Integrating Cross-Platform Components

INTRODUCTION

This chapter discusses how to build portable GUIs with integrated cross-platform components. We'll discuss the basics of cross-platform integration for client/server environments, the architecture of integration code for a typical cross-platform component, and how to generate the integration code using a macro processor.

In modern, open client/server environments, it is necessary that applications and components from multiple sources interoperate with one another. This chapter discusses how the db-UIM/X environment handles this issue.

WIDGETS AND SWIDGETS

In earlier chapters, we discussed widgets and referenced "swidgets." To integrate a widget, a *swidget* is needed . . . a "shadow widget" (or "inseparable companion"). UIM/X—the foundation of db-UIM/X—uses swidgets to hold the code and data it needs to manipulate widgets.

To integrate a cross-platform component a swidget is also needed, or, more specifically, a special type called an *adapter swidget*. This is used to connect UIM/X to the widgets in a cross-platform environment.

211

When integrating a widget, a developer needs to write the code that defines the swidget. This isn't necessary, however, when integrating a cross-platform component. UIM/X 2.6 includes a convenience function for creating adapter swidgets (convenience functions were discussed earlier in the book).

What is required is to write some integration code to wrap the cross-platform component in a UIM/X-compatible interface. UIM/X, via an adapter swidget, operates on the component through this interface.

The integration code presents the cross-platform component to UIM/X as if it were actually developed in UIM/X that is, the integration code gives the illusion of being the generated code for a UIM/X component.

UIM/X 2.6 includes some sample integration code as contributed software; the code is the actual integration code for the Cross-Platform Toolset components.

A cross-platform component defines a public interface as consisting of a constructor and a suite of methods. The methods set and retrieve property values, perform operations on the component, and register event procedures (callbacks).

To integrate a cross-platform, both a C and C++ version of a wrapper around the cross-platform component must be written. The C wrapper is a set of methods implemented using the UIM/X Method system, while the C++ wrapper is a C++ class.

The wrapper gives UIM/X and generated code a way to operate on the cross-platform component: UIM/X and the generated C code use the C wrapper, and generated C++ code uses the C++ wrapper. Figure 14.1 illustrates the wrapper code structure and how the interfaces are provided.

There are a number of tasks that must be accomplished to wrap a cross-platform component for integration with UIM/X.

- Writing the C wrapper constructor: This function is similar to the Interface Function of a UIM/X component. In UIM/X the name of this function is the value of an instance's Constructor property. UIM/X and generated code call the wrapper constructor to create instances of the component.

- Writing the C++ wrapper constructor: This is the same as above, but for C++ code.

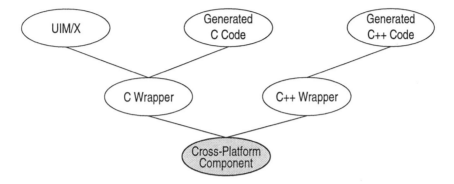

Figure 14.1 Wrapping a cross-platform component

- Writing the wrapper methods: These are functions that wrap the real methods of the cross-platform component and are used in UIM/X and in generated C code. (For some cross-platform components it is necessary to write wrapper methods that override methods inherited from the Interface base class.)

- Getting a class code for the cross-platform component: Class code is needed to be able to register methods for the component in the UIM/X system. UxNewInterfaceClassID() is used to get a class code for the base component class, and UxNewSubclassID() is used to get class codes for its subclasses. This creates a class hierarchy in UIM/X that parallels your cross-platform component class hierarchy and, in particular, allows methods to be inherited within UIM/X.

- Registering the wrapper method: This is done by calling UxMethod-Register() with the class code of the cross-platform component.

- Defining the context structure used by UIM/X to create subclasses of the cross-platform component must be done.

- Defining the C++ wrapper class: This class is used in generated C++ code and when the wrapper implementation itself is compiled; the member functions of the class wrap the real methods of the component. For some components, it is necessary to write member functions that override virtual member functions inherited from the Interface base class.

- Defining C and C++ bindings: These bindings are macros whose definitions are conditional on the language being used. The C bindings use the UIM/X Method System (UxMethodLookup()) to invoke the wrapper methods, while the C++ bindings call member functions of the component's wrapper class. The binding macros are used by UIM/X and by generated code to set and retrieve properties and to manipulate the component.

CREATING ADAPTER SWIDGETS

UIM/X handles all of the interface elements in a project using swidgets. Each component must have a constructor function that returns a swidget. When components are built inside of UIM/X this swidget is supplied by the generated code. For other components, the developer creates a special adapter swidget to connect UIM/X to the Motif elements in the components.

An adapter swidget is a special class of swidget representing an instance of a component in UIM/X. The adapter swidget holds on to the design-time swidget information (or, for generated code, run-time information), such as the class code used for method dispatch.

This class code is obtained by calling the functions UxNewInterface-ClassID() or UxNewSubclassID(), and methods are attached to the adapter swidget by registering those methods against this class code.

The function UxAdapterSwidget() is used to create an adapter swidget. This function requires a Motif widget (usually the controlling widget of the component) and a class code.

MANAGING INSTANCES

The C wrapper constructor must not manage (in the XT sense of the word) the widgets of the underlying component; UIM/X expects the C wrapper constructor to create the component, call UxAdapterSwidget(), and return an adapter swidget. At that point the component should have created its widgets, but not managed them.

UIM/X manages the component by invoking the method Interface_UxManage() on the component. Components inherit a version of this method from the Interface base class, but they can provide their own version if required.

DESIGNATING A CHILD SITE

Components that can accept children must define a childSite() method. This method designates a child site by returning the swidget whose widget can be used as the parent of the component's children.

A component's child site widget is usually the widget linked to the component's adapter swidget by UxAdapterSwidget(). If the child site widget is some other widget, another adapter swidget needs to be created for that widget.

CREATING INSTANCES OF COMPONENTS

In UIM/X Instances are created when one interface is reused in another. The interface being reused is called a component, and each use of that component is an Instance (this was discussed in Chapter 12).

When cross-platform components are integrated with UIM/X they can also be used as components. the developer can build an interface with components created elsewhere (including by other developers) and then reuse it by creating an Instance of it.

UIM/X calls the method UxCanBeAnInstance() to determine whether or not the developer can create an Instance of a component. If "False" is returned, then an Instance cannot be created. Any interface where the component is top-level cannot be used as an Instance. If "True" is returned, or if the component has no such method, UIM/X permits the creation of an Instance of the component.

DEFINING DESIGN-TIME METHODS

In addition to writing wrapper methods for a component's own methods, some methods for UIM/X may have to be implemented for internal use during design time. The adapter swidget forwards some design-time actions to the underlying component by translating them into methods. These design-time methods include the following.

- UxCheckChildren(): This determines whether or not the parent can accept the proposed children. By default, the method rejects children if the parent does not have a childSite() method.

- UxDrawhandles(). This draws selection handles on the component. By default, it draws the selection handles on the widget passed to UxAdapterSwidget().

- UxObjectToRecreate(): This specifies the object to recreate when the user edits one of the children of a component. By default, it returns the adapter swidget for the component.

The convenience function UxAdapterDesignMethods() must be used to register one or more of these methods.

ADDING EVENT PROCEDURES

Cross-platform components, such as those provided with the Cross-Platform Toolset, provide methods for registering event procedures. From the point of view of a component, an event procedure is like a property whose value happens to be a function pointer.

Event procedures can be added as properties by defining set and get accessors, but this would force the developer to define external functions and then enter function pointers directly into the Property Editor. A more elegant approach is to give access to an editor such as the UIM/X Callback Editor.

If the component has an event procedure with a signature different from the standard XT callback signature, a wrapper must be written to bridge the gap between the XT-style callback procedures and the actual event procedure defined by the component. This can be done because the call data argument of an XtCallbackProc is meant to be a structure holding whatever arguments a particular callback requires. For an event procedure with special arguments, the wrapper will transfer these arguments into a call data structure and pass them along to the user's callback.

The wrapper event procedure—not the callback function defined in the Callback Editor—is installed on the cross-platform component. When the event occurs, the component calls the wrapper procedure, which then composes a call to the user's callback function.

The following items are noted with respect to the event procedures.

1. To add an event procedure such as a Behavior property, it is necessary to define a special type of accessor method which is called a callback accessor. Callback accessors are named Add*EventName*-Proc(), where the *EventName* is the name of the event. In this method, an event procedure is registered with the component.

UIM/X examines the name of a method to determine whether or not it is an accessor method, as identified above.

2. A callback structure is defined to hold the arguments passed to the event procedure by the components.

3. The wrapper event procedure must be written so as to be registered by the callback accessor. This procedure stores the arguments received from the component in the callback structure and then composes a call to the user's callback function. The callback structure is passed as client data to the callback.

By performing the above steps, UIM/X is informed that the component has a property named *EventName* and that this property belongs in the Behavior category of the Property Editor. UIM/X then automatically makes the Callback Editor available for the property.

The job of the callback accessor is to install a wrapper event procedure on the cross-platform component. The method accepts an XtCallback-Proc pointer and a client data pointer, both of which must be passed on to the wrapper event procedure. The XtCallbackProc pointer is the callback defined by the user in the Callback Editor (Callback Editor examples were given in earlier chapters). The client data pointer is the context structure for the interface. This must be passed to the user's callback. UIM/X then uses it to give the user access to the interface-specific variables and the swidgets in the interface.

Both the callback and the client data must be passed on to the wrapper event procedure. If the component allows the passing of user data into the event procedure, the callback and the client data can be stored in a structure and passed as the user data. Alternatively, the X context manager can be used . . . the callback accessor would store the callback and client data, and the wrapper event procedure can retrieve it later.

The way in which a callback structure is defined for each event type that passes special arguments to the user's event procedure is shown in the code below. In the wrapper event procedure, the callback structure is used to pass arguments as call data to the user's callback function. For example, the following callback structure is defined for the KeyDown, KeyUp, and KeyPress events of a Text Box:

```
typedef struct xk_key_cb_data {
    unsigned char char_code;
    short key;
    short state;
} XkKeyEventCallbackData;
```

It is necessary to have a wrapper event procedure only if the event procedure's signature doesn't match XtCallbackProc. The job of the wrapper event procedure is to build a callback structure containing its arguments and then call the given callback.

THE INTEGRATION CODE AND AUGMENTING UIM/X

The integration code for a cross-platform component consists of a header file and a source file, with the header file containing the following elements:

- C and C++ bindings for the wrapper methods
- definition of the context structure
- definition of the C++ wrapper class
- declaration for the C wrapper constructor

and the source file containing:

- wrapper functions for the C bindings of methods
- wrapper class constructor
- C wrapper constructor
- registration of the wrapper methods

When integration code is being written, the DESIGN_TIME macro can be used to distinguish between design-time and run-time code. Design-time code is code that should only be compiled when it is desired to augment UIM/X (discussed below), and run-time code is code that should not be compiled and linked with UIM/X.

Once integration code for the cross-platform components has been prepared, the next step is to build an augmented UIM/X. This gives users the ability to create instances of previously designed cross-platform components. A set of steps (described in the db-UIM/X *Developer's Guide*) involves editing makefile macros and managing working directories.

SUMMARY

There are other steps involved in the cross-platform component process—creating a customized palette, writing code to integrate each of the components with UIM/X, and generating the integration code. These steps are described in detail in the various db-UIM/X documentation volumes.

The important thing for the reader to grasp is that the db-UIM/X environment can be used as the integration mechanism for a number of components, both those developed using db-UIM/X and those from other sources. The same development paradigms that are used to develop applications (as described in earlier chapters) apply to this process.

Appendices

Appendix A

Client/Server Future Trends

CLIENT/SERVER APPLICATIONS DEPLOYMENT[*]

During the middle to late 1980s, personal productivity application of computer technology spread rapidly with the advent of affordable desktop computers and good application software for word processing, desktop publishing, and spreadsheets. In the early 1990s, departmental client/server applications began to emerge with groupware applications such as Lotus Notes and client/server application development tools such as PowerBuilder. As we move into the mid to late 1990s, we will see the full emergence of client/server implementations across the enterprise—and even intraenterprise. This is seen in the emergence of applications such as the World Wide Web and more powerful application development tools such as db-UIM/X.

The emergence of client/server implementation has been made possible by the technology evolution discussed previously in this book. The future is fundamentally built on the client/server architecture.

In the past, the "production-level" systems implemented in large organizations were done on mainframes for internal applications such as payroll and order entry. Personal computers were used to deploy personal productivity solutions. Today, the worldwide competitive marketplace is forcing organizations of every size and type to connect to the outside world. It is no longer feasible to make order entry an internal function. It

---

[*] This appendix supplied courtesy of Bluestone, the db-UIM/X vendor.

223

is no longer feasible to develop products without the help of external partners. The old style of computing architecture has to change to embrace the new organizational challenges of interacting with the external world in a real-time manner.

Production-level client/server applications are being deployed in large and small organizations around the globe. These applications support distributed databases, multiple processing locations, and a variety of highly intuitive interfaces. With all of this complexity, businesses are finding that there are tremendous paybacks to be gained by implementing these client/server systems. The benefits come in the form of improved business processes, closer ties to customers, and reduced time to market for new products.

Organizations are not only deploying their own applications, but commercial off-the-shelf (COTS) products are also moving toward a client/server architecture. Lotus Notes has been the vanguard of this type of application—letting virtual teams work together across organizational and geographical boundaries.

Finally, millions of people are using client/server implementations every day across the Internet and the World Wide Web. Client/server architecture will be the foundation, as the Internet matures to a forum for conducting business and the World Wide Web matures from a network of only documents to one of interactive documents and applications.

EMERGING CLIENT/SERVER TECHNOLOGY TRENDS

With the increased use of client/server architectures, there is enormous pressure to increase the timeliness of application delivery and the productivity of software developers. Two major software trends that will occur are the increased ease of development and the increased availability of shrink-wrapped applications containing client/server capabilities. Another major trend is increased network availability.

NETWORK AVAILABILITY

The growth of the Internet, along with the increased availability of intraorganizational LANs and WANs provides the network infrastucture that allows software to take advantage of client/server architectures. Networking has become available and inexpensive. Combined with urgent business needs, internal development and shrink-wrapped applications are rushing to take advantage of the resources on the network. Internally, this removes the walls between organizations since they are now capable of effectively sharing data. Externally, this opens up new markets and permits closer ties to customers, suppliers, and partners.

The Internet is based on a distributed network architecture, conducive to change and rapid growth. It is likely to serve as the major logical backbone of interenterprise communications over the next century. However, the entire infrastructure from "on-ramps" to "highways" will change and evolve to increase the capacity to handle larger volumes of users and increased data needs from multimedia. Huge amounts of infrastructure are being invested in today—from fiber-optics networks to cellular communications and satellite transmissions. This investment will lay the foundation for instantaneous access to consumers, customers, suppliers, and partners. Major companies will take advantage of this logical backbone to deliver client/server applications that are truly global in nature.

As the World Wide Web evolves, today's issues of security and bandwidth will be resolved, allowing for production-level transactions to occur over the public networks. Consumers will be able to purchase goods from electronic storefronts, and businesses will be able to conduct business over public networks.

Web "browsers" will emerge into a powerful user interface that will contain applications beyond simple browsing. In addition, live production-level applications will be able to be built on the Web.

At this writing, Bluestone is building a follow-on tool to db-UIM/X that will facilitate application development over the World Wide Web (and even for internal client/server applications). This development tool will "bind" HTML Objects (the standard user-interface language for the Web, standing for Hypertext Markup Language) to other objects—including database, function, executable, or file. In future versions, this tool will also connect to multiple object systems such as OLE and CORBA. The different object types can reside on computers across the entire Internet—all working together as if they were directly on the end-user's screen. This level of ease of development and deployment is the hallmark of the emerging client/server applications.

OBJECT TECHNOLOGY

From a software perspective, the idea of reusable objects has been a siren song for several years now. Fortunately, the technology is maturing, and will become very powerful over the next five years. Not only will it become more powerful, but ease of use and incorporation of this technology in applications will become prevalent.

There are several factors of object technology that will emerge, as discussed below.

Objects

Objects are pieces of reusable code. Objects are becoming well defined with emerging standards for SmallTalk and C++—primary languages today for raw object development. In addition, well-defined standards are also emerging for classic programming languages such as C. For example, the Object Management Group's first specification for their Common Object Request Broker Architecture was based on a C-level API—opening up the world of objects and object definition to C.

Clear definition of objects spawns the commercial development of reusable objects. Windowing environments have had defined object systems for years. For example, Motif has a base set of 35 objects. But out of this core GUI object definition, others have been able to make hundreds of commercial add-on objects for Motif. This is also seen in the Windows world. Visual Basic, for example, has a clear definition of what objects are and how they are integrated—creating a market for hundreds of add-on VBXs.

Objects will increase beyond the GUI space. Already, there are large numbers of objects libraries available for common systems services such as file, print, and even databases. In addition, business objects are starting to be defined within organizations. These can take many forms, including database stored procedures, C++ class libraries, or even pieces of legacy code. With the creation of standard interfaces, it becomes easier to wrap software into reusable objects.

Today, millions of dollars are being spent on development of these objects. For example, Taligent has nearly 200 developers devoted to the task of creating a library of over 1,000 objects for reuse on multiple platforms. These prebuilt objects will be leveraged by thousands of other developers building on the core functionality they provide "out of the box."

Object Request Brokers and Object Middleware

With the advent of reusable objects, there is a need for object systems to evolve in order to make objects readily available to one another across complex networks. Object request brokers are emerging as the "middleware"—connecting objects to each other.

At the simple end of object middleware is OLE (Object Linking and Embedding) from Microsoft. This technology lets developers and users link objects of different types. For example, a spreadsheet object can be linked to a word processing document—with data and calculations updating each "object."

The Object Management Group has taken this a step further with the CORBA standard. CORBA is now in its second version of specification. It not only defines how objects interact, but it also defines the fact that they seamlessly work across networks.

An emerging technology of object middleware is software that permits multiple object systems to work together. For example, OLE objects only know about other OLE objects. New object middleware will allow any object to interact with any other object. An OLE object, for example, could use a DSOM (IBM's Distributed System Object Model). Visual Edge Software has announced a technology called Object Bridge to facilitate just this type of interaction.

Object middleware is still in an infancy state. CORBA V2 has recently been defined, but commercial implementations are more than a year away. It will take several more years for commerical technology to fulfill the promise of distributed objects working together over distributed networks of computers. As this maturation occurs, developers and end users will be able to take advantage of the power of reusable objects in a manner similar to the way electrical engineers take advantage of reusable components such as complex integrated circuits made up of millions of transistors with greatly simplified interfaces.

As with objects, major developments are underway. Leading hardware and software vendors are racing to come to market with more functional, robust, and production-quality object middleware. IBM, SUN, HP, Digital, and Microsoft are being joined by many nimble high-technology companies such as Iona and Visual Edge to create this next generation of foundation infrastructure technology.

Object Development

Visual programming will become the dominant development methodology over the next decade. Popular visual programming tools such as PowerBuilder and db-UIM/X have emerged to enable developers to create objects graphically and bind these objects together. CASE tools such as

SoftBench give developers the ability to graphically search for objects and look at how they work. Even end-user applications such as Microsoft Word come with the ability to link different object types. This will result in quantum leaps of productivity as objects become more robust, more useful, and better defined as accessible network objects.

Bob Bickel
March 1995

Appendix B

ProtoGen+ Client/Server Suite 5.0

ProtoGen+ Client/Server Suite[*] has been built with three concepts in mind: productivity, speed of deployed application, and team programming. We have been developing this environment that you are using today for the last 6½ years. Our development team built this environment to give the developer productivity through the use of:

- object-oriented programming
- visual programming
- software components
- project management

The end result of a visual programming session with ProtoGen+ is code generation. We generate object-oriented code for Microsoft Foundation Classes (MFC), Borland's ObjectWindows Library (OWL), and ANSI C. Our generators create 16- or 32-bit code for Windows, Windows NT, and the most current version of Windows 95 as of the publication of this book.

By making it easy to build user interfaces, database programming, and business logic, we have seen unprecedented development of complex Windows applications by even casual developers.

---

[*] The material in Chapters 4 through 8 examined version 4.0 of the ProtoGen+ Client/ Server Suite. This appendix has been provided for those readers interested in learning more about the next version of the product set—expected to be available around publication time of this book—courtesy of the vendors.

Team programming and project management have been incorporated into the tool to work naturally, the way developers work. We have both vertical and horizontal team development, as well as a Manage Project Files screen for viewing all components of an application across a network.

The ProtoGen+ Client/Server Suite consists of best-of-breed components in one cohesive, naturally flowing environment. ProtoView Development created most of the components of ProtoGen+ and then partnered with the best software companies to provide database drivers, report writing capabilities, a version control system, and a graphics library to round out the suite.

The ProtoGen+ Client/Server Suite consists of:

- **ProtoGen+**—the workbench and code generators
- **WinControl**—data entry software components
- **DataTable**—grid/spreadsheet component
- **SQLView**—data access methods through Visual Database Programming and APIs
- **INTERSOLV ODBC Drivers**—23 data drivers for PC and SQL databases
- **Crystal Report Writer Pro and Visual Coder**—creates reports and has a UI for point and click options to link reports to the application and define code generation options
- **Graphic Server and Visual Coder**—uses point and click methods to create 13 different graphs from static data in your application, data from our DataTable, or data from the DBMS
- **Version Control**—total integration to PVCS for software version control (PVCS is not included)

TEAM PROGRAMMING

We have created the tool to work with two methodologies for team development. The first methodology is vertical team development where the project is broken up into subsystems or screens. Here, ten screens might be assigned to one developer and ten screens to another developer. Each developer creates the user interface, business logic, and database access for their subsystem or screens. ProtoGen+ then allows these subsystems to be integrated and connected using visual programming techiques.

The second methodology is horizontal team development. Using this technique the best coders write the business logic, the best database programmer or DBA writes the database access logic, and the best screen designers create the user interface (UI). ProtoGen+ Client/Server Suite also has excellent integration with PVCS.

Now that we have defined the objective or methodology, let's see how it works in the ProtoGen+ Client/Server Suite.

VERTICAL TEAM DEVELOPMENT

When starting the project, select DLL code generation (see Figure B.1). We have advanced support for both static (user DLL) and dynamic (extension DLL) creation. Static DLL creation adds the OWL or MFC class library to your current DLL. Dynamic DLL creation dynamically links to the MFC or OWL class libraries. If you have more than one DLL or subsystem in your application, we recommend using dynamic DLL creation.

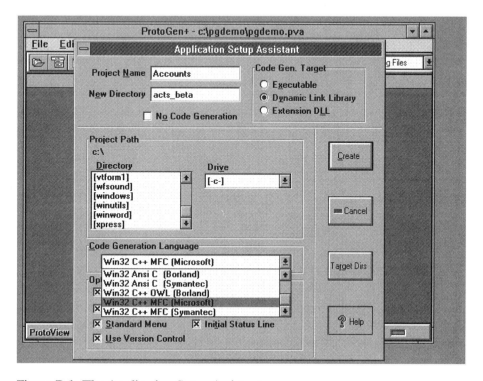

Figure B.1 The Application Setup Assistant screen

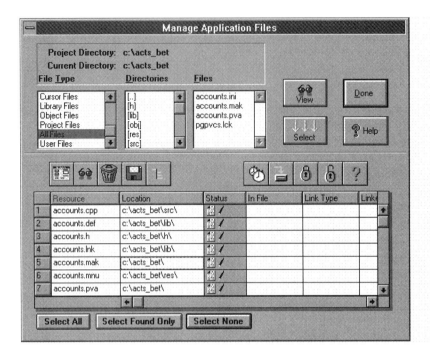

Figure B.2 The Manage Application Files screen

Working independently from others in your group, you can interactively create menus, forms, database access, and user logic. At the end of the week or when you hit a milestone in your development, you check in your files against the network version control system. This is done through the Manage Application Files screen (see Figure B.2). The Manage Application Files screen shows you the status, location, and file type of the sources of the project you are working on. At a glance this gives the developer the description of each file in the application.

Use the following toolbar in the Manage Application Files screen to implement version control as it is integrated with the ProtoGen+ Client/Server Suite.

You can use the Manage Application Files screen to set options for the version control system. The first thing you need to do in a team environment is to set the archive directory on the network. In order for project synchronization to work in a team environment, this has to be a network drive. You may set it to a local drive if you are developing an application by yourself. Usually the project leader would use the "Stamp Version" button to mark the source files with a version label to create a build. This eliminates the project leader from going to each source module to mark it with a version label. ProtoGen+ already knows all the components, so it is easy to mark each one. You may also create version labels from this screen that can be used by the developers when checking in software.

You can synchronize the project with other members on the team. Over time, other members on the team will be adding features, fixing bugs, and cleaning up their code or the subsystem they are working on. By clicking on the Synchronize button, ProtoGen+ will go out to the network and retrieve the latest revision of software from other members of the team. By using this button, you easily can bring the project up to date with other members of the team.

As you reach stages of completion of your software, fixing bugs, or completing features, you would check in your modules. This also helps other members of the team get the latest version of the project when they use the Synchronize Project option.

Using the Check In button, you can check in a single file or a series of files. We added one-step check in, with smart features for checking in only files that changed. This will check in sources that you have modified only and unlock the sources that you did not change. You also have the ability to force a check in, even if the module has not changed. Using "Ignore Changes on Check In" will unlock your current source modules and move your set of sources back to the last revision. This feature would be used if you added code that created too much instability in the product or if you wanted to start again from the last check in.

The Check Out Sources or Get button allows you to retrieve one or more source files from the version control system. You may check out the most recent revision of the software or a version label of the software. The Check Out Read-Only WorkFile option allows you to build and view the current set of software, but not change it or lock it. This allows other developers to check the software for development.

If you choose Check Out Writable WorkFile with a Lock, this will lock the source module, allowing only you to change the modules. This prevents other members of the team from updating the software when you are working on it.

Version labels are a way to assign a name or label to an instance of a source module or revision of a source module. This allows easy extraction from the version control system to create a build of the software at a specific point of the development cycle.

The Information button shows the developer the history of a current source module. This includes revision comments, dates and revision numbers, and labels. In addition, the file information screen also allows you to add, delete, and change version labels for this file.

DLL Code Generation

ProtoGen+ makes it easy to create dynamic link libraries (DLLs). ProtoGen+ works with a PVA file. A PVA file is our project file. It keeps track of the application screen links, source modules, resources, and many other pieces of information describing the application that you build through ProtoGen+'s Visual Programming capabilities. In a vertical team programming scenario, the project leader would create an application EXE, which is one PVA file to ProtoGen+. Each member of the team would create a separate PVA, which will be a DLL for each subsystem.

Creating a DLL is easy in ProtoGen+. It requires you to choose between static DLL and extension DLL at code generation time. The benefits of DLL creation are:

- modular design

- easier maintenance

- memory efficiency

- reuse of code, database access, and user interface

To generate code for DLLs, you select the Generate button [[]] from the ProtoGen+ toolbar. This will generate all the code for the current design. Selecting from the menu choice Build->Generate Full will show the screen illustrated in Figure B.3, allowing you to make choices about the kind of DLL that is generated.

ProtoGen+ Code Generation

The end result of a visual programming session is code generation. ProtoGen+ Client/Server Suite contains 16- and 32-bit code generation for

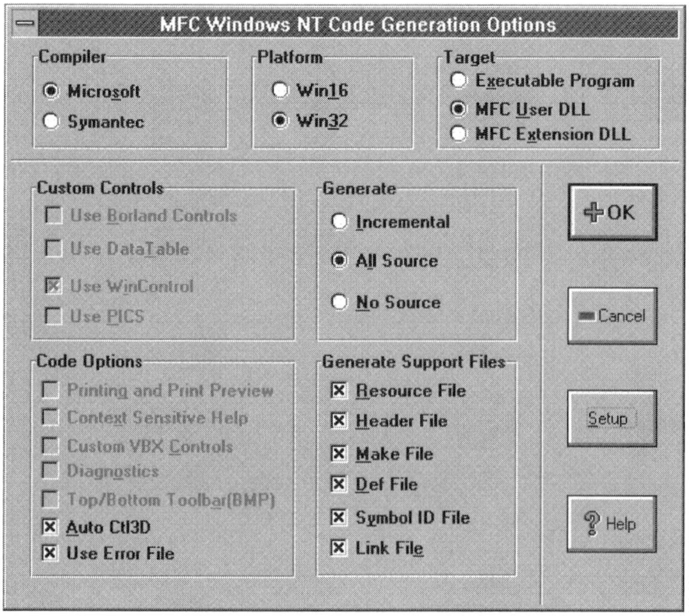

Figure B.3 The MFC Windows NT Code Generation Options screen

ANSI C, MFC, and OWL. The compilers supported are Microsoft, Borland, Symantec, and Watcom.

ProtoGen+ has regeneration technology built into each generator. Code regeneration gives the developer the ability to insert code into the source code and not lose the code when regenerating. The developer also has the ability to lock files and sections of the generated code. This allows the developer to change the code that is generated. ProtoGen+ handles code regeneration by placing "//Regen_XXXX" comments in the code. The developer then places his or her code between these two points for code preservation. Figure B.4 shows a code snippet of MFC-generated code with code regeneration comments in the code. The screen also shows our new ProtoView Programming Assistant.

The ProtoView Programming Assistant is a full-featured code editor that is integrated with the ProtoGen+ Workbench for easy access to code from the user interface. By right-clicking over the user interface, ProtoGen+ will place you at the exact position in your source module to add code to the application (see Figure B.5).

The ProtoView Programming Assistant supports advanced features such as Color Syntax Highlighting, multifile searches, keyboard macros,

```
hWinCtl = LoadLibrary(WINCTL_LIB);

if(hWinCtl < (HINSTANCE)HINSTANCE_ERROR)
    ::MessageBox(NULL, "Unable to load WinCtl",
            "System Error", MB_OK | MB_ICONSTOP);

vwConnectApplication(m_hInstance, m_pszAppName, 0);
//Regen_MainInit
//Regen_MainInit

Ctl3dAutoSubclass(m_hInstance);        // Initialize Ctl3D Support

//lRegen_MainRun
//lRegen_MainRun
// create main MDI Frame window
pMainFrame =  new CMainWindow;
if (!pMainFrame->LoadFrame(ACT_MAIN))
    return FALSE;
pMainFrame->ShowWindow(m_nCmdShow);
pMainFrame->UpdateWindow();
m_pMainWnd = pMainFrame;

//Regen_MainExit
//Regen_MainExit
```

Figure B.4 The ProtoView Programming Assistant screen

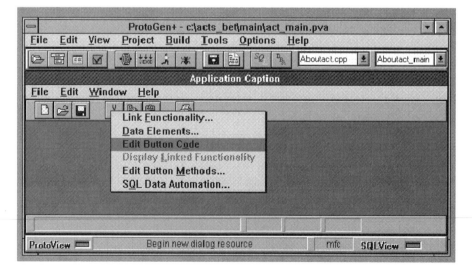

Figure B.5 The ProtoGen+ Workbench screen

undo, right mouse clicks to edit source from an "#include 'myheader.h'" source module, and MDI document support.

WRITE ONLY SOME USER CODE

ProtoGen+ can build 100 percent of the user-interface code and 80 to 100 percent of the database code visually. Using our data automation technology, you can perform actions on button events, double clicks, and other user-interface events to move data and perform database actions.

DATABASE

One of the most important features of this release is the Database Visual Programming aspect of the product. From ProtoGen+'s toolbar you have direct access to all the database functionality of the application you are building (see Figure B.6).

From this screen you may create database SQL statements or results sets for your application. Each database action has a name that you define. The database actions include validation lists, which may be used for exit and enter validation for a field. You may define search methods, joins, updates, deletes, adds, and execute stored procedures. Editing a result set definition allows you to use point and click methods to create SQL statements.

Through data automation you can perform database actions on events. Visually you attach these database actions to enter and exit events to fields and screens. You may also have a series of events that may take place before a screen is displayed and destroyed. From ViewPaint, ProtoGen+'s dialog editor, you may select data automation statements or create them. Depending on the type of field you are working with, you have a selection of different data automation options that you may apply. For string controls, editboxes, date controls, and other fields, you may use the following

Figure B.6 ProGen+'s toolbar

screen to apply database actions for validation, exit field lookups, and execute database automation methods.

The user-interface designer may create a form by selecting fields from a tools palette, creating a form from an existing database, or using an existing result set definition. The result set definition can be as simple as one view of one database or as complex as multiple joins, one-to-many relationships, and BLOB fields or binary data. This allows the database designer to create the correct view of the table and the user-interface design.

Visually you may create "Parent Data" relationships. In one form you have a customer ID as the key field with customer information. In the same form you can have a DataTable with a list of invoices linked to that customer ID. This describes a one-to-many relationship. Visually you can link a form to the DataTable or list of invoices. By double-clicking on the list (DataTable) you bring up a form with that line item of invoice data. When the data are updated in the second form, they are communicated back to the prior form's list (DataTable). These types of "Parent Data" relationships are all handled through Visual Programming!

In addition to a Forms Assistant, the Workbench also has a DataBase Assistant to help create database tables, columns, and indexes.

ProtoGen+ comes with complete C++ classes for all the visual aspects of database programming. This gives the developer complete control of the application coding using the latest in object-oriented techniques.

VISUAL PROGRAMMING

You can attach functionality to listboxes, comboboxes, and DataTables through double-click events. You now can attach functionality to menus on Dialogs and MDI Windows.

We have also added drag-drop support to controls, playing wave files for help and error messages, visual linking of context-sensitive help, and tool tips. These properties can easily be set just by clicking the mouse.

Two new controls have been added to the package: an indented line control for displaying horizontally or vertically indented lines and a new button control for creating toolbar buttons.

New and improved support for dialogs is also featured. Upon starting a new screen or dialog, you may choose from a list of standard dialog templates to which you can add. You also can attach icons and menus to the dialogs. Through the workbench you can change the dialog class inheritance to allow for reuse of dialog box and data entry form logic.

NEW GRAPHIC VISUAL CODER

You can visually graph data from a DataTable, static data, or from a DBMS by using result set definitions or creating your own.

REPORT WRITER VISUAL CODER

You can easily create reports with Crystal Reports Pro 4.0. Using our Report Writer Visual Coder, you can link reports to your user interface, customize the report, see it work live in test mode, and generate code for that report.

DATATABLE SPREADSHEET GRID CONTROL

By using the DataTable, you can display views of data from SQL queries and multiple databases. It has easy-to-use setup dialog screens for configuring the DataTable exactly the way you want. Some of the new features in the DataTable are the ability to split the screen vertically and horizontally in order to create independent scrolling regions. Built-in column summing and the display of pictures or bitmaps in cells are also supported (see Figure B.7).

	Resource	Location	Status	In File	Link Type	Link
1	Aboutdean	c:\acts_bet\dean\res\		dean.dlg	Menu Dlg:	&Ab
2	backgrnd	c:\acts_bet\dean\res\		maindlg.dlg	Unlinked	
3	DTDialog	c:\acts_bet\dean\res\		dt_dlgs.dlg	Unlinked	
4	pic	c:\acts_bet\dean\res\		pict.dlg	Unlinked	
5	pict	c:\acts_bet\dean\res\		pict.dlg	Unlinked	
6	StatusLine	c:\acts_bet\dean\res\		toolbars.dlg	Bottom Toolbar	
7	TopToolbar	c:\acts_bet\dean\res\		toolbars.dlg	Top Toolbar	

Figure B.7 DataTable features

SUMMARY

The use of component technology, controls, visual database programming, code generation, properties, easy editing of code for adding user logic, and a scalable and open architecture make ProtoGen+ Client/Server Suite the best choice for building database and client/server applications in today's complex environments.

ProtoView Development is located at 2540 Route 130, Cranbury, NJ 08512; telephone: (609) 655-5000; fax: (609) 655-5353, 1-800-231-8588.

Appendix C

Client/Server and Middleware Product Checklists

This section contains checklists and forms that should be used when evaluating products under consideration for your environment. By filling in the blanks on the following pages a great deal of the client/server and middleware evaluation process can be undertaken, and the results from this research can lead directly into the product selection phase.

As with any product selection process, it is strongly recommended that you evaluate several different products for each of the areas that are to be part of your client/server environment: development tools, database gateways, workflow engines, directory service managers, security managers, etc. Sufficient space is provided for several different products within each of the areas you are likely to be evaluating.

APPLICATION DEVELOPMENT TOOL

Product 1

Product Name: _____

Vendor: _____

Current Version: _____

Platform(s): _____

Product History (when first released, etc.)

_____
_____

Visual Programming Capabilities (describe)

_____
_____
_____
_____

Client Side Development (describe, evaluate)

_____
_____
_____
_____
_____
_____
_____

Server Side Development (describe, evaluate)

_____
_____
_____
_____
_____
_____
_____

Product 1 *(continued)*

Application Partitioning Capabilities (describe, evaluate) _____

_____

_____

_____

_____

_____

_____

_____

Team Development Capabilities (describe, evaluate) _____

_____

_____

_____

_____

_____

_____

_____

Comments and Evaluation from Reference Sites _____

_____

_____

_____

_____

_____

_____

_____

Next Version Expected _____

Major Enhancements _____

Product 1 *(continued)*

Middleware Interfaces (list and describe)   _____

_____

_____

_____

_____

_____

_____

_____

_____

Comments from Periodicals, Market Consultants, Other Sources (including
ratings, major capabilities versus competitors, shortcomings, etc.)

_____

_____

_____

_____

_____

_____

_____

_____

_____

_____

_____

_____

_____

_____

_____

_____

_____

_____

APPLICATION DEVELOPMENT TOOL

Product 2

Product Name: _____

Vendor: _____

Current Version: _____

Platform(s): _____

Product History (when first released, etc.)
_____
_____

Visual Programming Capabilities (describe)
_____
_____
_____
_____

Client Side Development (describe, evaluate)
_____
_____
_____
_____
_____
_____
_____

Server Side Development (describe, evaluate)
_____
_____
_____
_____
_____
_____
_____

Product 2 *(continued)*

Application Partitioning Capabilities (describe, evaluate)

_____
_____
_____
_____
_____
_____
_____

Team Development Capabilities (describe, evaluate)

_____
_____
_____
_____
_____
_____
_____

Comments and Evaluation from Reference Sites

_____
_____
_____
_____
_____
_____
_____

Next Version Expected _____

Major Enhancements _____

Product 2 *(continued)*

Middleware Interfaces (list and describe) _____

_____
_____
_____
_____
_____
_____
_____
_____
_____

Comments from Periodicals, Market Consultants, Other Sources (including ratings, major capabilities versus competitors, shortcomings, etc.)

_____
_____
_____
_____
_____
_____
_____
_____
_____
_____
_____
_____
_____
_____
_____
_____
_____
_____
_____
_____
_____
_____

APPLICATION DEVELOPMENT TOOL

Product 3

Product Name: _____

Vendor: _____

Current Version: _____

Platform(s): _____

Product History (when first released, etc.)

_____
_____

Visual Programming Capabilities (describe)

_____
_____
_____
_____

Client Side Development (describe, evaluate)

_____
_____
_____
_____
_____
_____

Server Side Development (describe, evaluate)

_____
_____
_____
_____
_____
_____

Product 3 *(continued)*

Application Partitioning Capabilities (describe, evaluate)

_____
_____
_____
_____
_____
_____
_____

Team Development Capabilities (describe, evaluate)

_____
_____
_____
_____
_____
_____
_____

Comments and Evaluation from Reference Sites

_____
_____
_____
_____
_____
_____
_____

Next Version Expected _____

Major Enhancements _____

Product 3 *(continued)*

Middleware Interfaces (list and describe) _____

_____
_____
_____
_____
_____
_____
_____
_____
_____
_____

Comments from Periodicals, Market Consultants, Other Sources (including ratings, major capabilities versus competitors, shortcomings, etc.)

_____
_____
_____
_____
_____
_____
_____
_____
_____
_____
_____
_____
_____
_____
_____
_____
_____
_____
_____
_____
_____
_____

MIDDLEWARE

Product 1

Product Name: _____

Vendor: _____

Current Version: _____

Platform(s): _____

Product History (when first released, etc.)
_____
_____

Service Area Supported (e.g., database, directory services, security, etc.)
_____
_____

Development Capabilities (describe, evaluate)
_____
_____
_____
_____
_____
_____
_____

Comments and Evaluation from Reference Sites
_____
_____
_____
_____
_____
_____
_____

Product 1 *(continued)*

Next Version Expected _____

Major Enhancements _____

Development Tool Interfaces (list and describe)

_____

_____

_____

_____

_____

_____

_____

_____

_____

_____

_____

_____

_____

Comments from Periodicals, Market Consultants, Other Sources (including ratings, major capabilities versus competitors, shortcomings, etc.)

_____

_____

_____

_____

_____

_____

_____

_____

_____

_____

_____

_____

_____

_____

_____

_____

_____

MIDDLEWARE

Product 2

Product Name: _____

Vendor: _____

Current Version: _____

Platform(s): _____

Product History (when first released, etc.)

_____
_____

Service Area Supported (e.g., database, directory services, security, etc.)

_____
_____

Development Capabilities (describe, evaluate)

_____
_____
_____
_____
_____
_____
_____

Comments and Evaluation from Reference Sites

_____
_____
_____
_____
_____
_____
_____

Product 2 *(continued)*

Next Version Expected _____

Major Enhancements _____

Development Tool Interfaces (list and describe)

_____
_____
_____
_____
_____
_____
_____
_____
_____
_____
_____
_____
_____
_____

Comments from Periodicals, Market Consultants, Other Sources (including ratings, major capabilities versus competitors, shortcomings, etc.)

_____
_____
_____
_____
_____
_____
_____
_____
_____
_____
_____
_____
_____
_____
_____
_____
_____
_____
_____
_____

Middleware

Product 3

Product Name: _____

Vendor: _____

Current Version: _____

Platform(s): _____

Product History (when first released, etc.)
_____
_____

Service Area Supported (e.g., database, directory services, security, etc.)
_____
_____

Development Capabilities (describe, evaluate)
_____
_____
_____
_____
_____
_____
_____

Comments and Evaluation from Reference Sites
_____
_____
_____
_____
_____
_____
_____

Product 3 *(continued)*

Next Version Expected _____

Major Enhancements _____

Development Tool Interfaces (list and describe)

_____
_____
_____
_____
_____
_____
_____
_____
_____
_____
_____
_____
_____
_____

Comments from Periodicals, Market Consultants, Other Sources (including ratings, major capabilities versus competitors, shortcomings, etc.)

_____
_____
_____
_____
_____
_____
_____
_____
_____
_____
_____
_____
_____
_____
_____
_____
_____
_____
_____

MIDDLEWARE

Product 4

Product Name: _____

Vendor: _____

Current Version: _____

Platform(s): _____

Product History (when first released, etc.)
_____
_____

Service Area Supported (e.g., database, directory services, security, etc.)
_____
_____

Development Capabilities (describe, evaluate)
_____
_____
_____
_____
_____
_____
_____

Comments and Evaluation from Reference Sites
_____
_____
_____
_____
_____
_____
_____

Product 4 *(continued)*

Next Version Expected _____

Major Enhancements _____

Development Tool Interfaces (list and describe)

Comments from Periodicals, Market Consultants, Other Sources (including ratings, major capabilities versus competitors, shortcomings, etc.)

Middleware

Product 5

Product Name: _____

Vendor: _____

Current Version: _____

Platform(s): _____

Product History (when first released, etc.)

_____

_____

Service Area Supported (e.g., database, directory services, security, etc.)

_____

_____

Development Capabilities (describe, evaluate)

_____

_____

_____

_____

_____

_____

_____

Comments and Evaluation from Reference Sites

_____

_____

_____

_____

_____

_____

_____

Product 5 *(continued)*

Next Version Expected _____

Major Enhancements _____

Development Tool Interfaces (list and describe)

_____
_____
_____
_____
_____
_____
_____
_____
_____
_____
_____
_____
_____
_____
_____

Comments from Periodicals, Market Consultants, Other Sources (including ratings, major capabilities versus competitors, shortcomings, etc.)

_____
_____
_____
_____
_____
_____
_____
_____
_____
_____
_____
_____
_____
_____
_____
_____
_____
_____
_____
_____

MIDDLEWARE

Product 6

Product Name: _____

Vendor: _____

Current Version: _____

Platform(s): _____

Product History (when first released, etc.)
_____
_____

Service Area Supported (e.g., database, directory services, security, etc.)
_____
_____

Development Capabilities (describe, evaluate)
_____
_____
_____
_____
_____
_____

Comments and Evaluation from Reference Sites
_____
_____
_____
_____
_____
_____

Product 6 *(continued)*

Next Version Expected _____

Major Enhancements _____

Development Tool Interfaces (list and describe)

_____
_____
_____
_____
_____
_____
_____
_____
_____
_____
_____
_____
_____
_____
_____

Comments from Periodicals, Market Consultants, Other Sources (including ratings, major capabilities versus competitors, shortcomings, etc.)

_____
_____
_____
_____
_____
_____
_____
_____
_____
_____
_____
_____
_____
_____
_____
_____
_____
_____
_____

MIDDLEWARE

Product 7

Product Name: _____

Vendor: _____

Current Version: _____

Platform(s): _____

Product History (when first released, etc.)
_____
_____

Service Area Supported (e.g., database, directory services, security, etc.)
_____
_____

Development Capabilities (describe, evaluate)
_____
_____
_____
_____
_____
_____
_____

Comments and Evaluation from Reference Sites
_____
_____
_____
_____
_____
_____
_____

Product 7 *(continued)*

Next Version Expected _____

Major Enhancements _____

Development Tool Interfaces (list and describe)

_____
_____
_____
_____
_____
_____
_____
_____
_____
_____
_____
_____
_____
_____
_____

Comments from Periodicals, Market Consultants, Other Sources (including ratings, major capabilities versus competitors, shortcomings, etc.)

_____
_____
_____
_____
_____
_____
_____
_____
_____
_____
_____
_____
_____
_____
_____
_____
_____
_____

Index